S0-CDV-959

MURDER FOLLOWED BY SUICIDE

By the same author:

PSYCHICAL RESEARCH TODAY
ELEVEN LOURDES MIRACLES
THE HABITUAL PRISONER
HOMOSEXUALITY

Publisher's Note: This series is continuous with the Cambridge Studies in Criminology, Volumes I to XIX, published by Macmillan & Co. London.

Contents

v

Mauin P. Om

D. J. West

MURDER

FOLLOWED BY SUICIDE

An inquiry carried out for
The Institute of Criminology, Cambridge

HARVARD UNIVERSITY PRESS

CAMBRIDGE, MASSACHUSETTS

1966

© D. J. West 1965

Printed in Great Britain

Acknowledgements

SPECIAL thanks are due to the Home Office, the Criminal Record Office, and to Dr Gavin Thurston, Secretary to the Coroners' Society, and numerous other coroners, who allowed us to see the documentary records on which this study is based. In addition, we are greatly indebted to many doctors, hospital authorities and social workers for answering questions and supplying information. In the preparation of the report, valuable advice has been given by the Home Office, and in particular by Mrs E. Gibson and Mr S. Klein, whose own study of murder in England provided an essential background to this more specialized inquiry.

Finally, we are greatly indebted to the three assistants who have worked on the project at various times: Mr Peter Didcot, who helped with some of the data counts, Mrs Derek Smedley, who abstracted records from Scotland Yard, and Miss C. H. Oppenheim, who interviewed the family doctors and other informants and prepared a preliminary analysis of the murder-suicide sample.

D. J. WEST

1965

I

Background to the Present Inquiry

In March 1964 a London newspaper gave prominence to the story of how a young man called at a house one morning and found the family of six all dead. Five of the bodies had severe head wounds or other marks of violent death, but the sixth, that of the husband, showed no visible injuries. The police were reported to have said that no one, apart from the husband, was connected with the deaths. Such examples of family carnage, though fortunately in themselves rare occurrences, make a substantial contribution to the murder rate. Since murders are counted by the number of bodies, this single affair, if found to be a murder incident, would increase the statistics of murder for the year by at least 3%.

In round figures, the number of suicides each year in England and Wales is 5,000, the number of murders 150, of which 50 are murders followed by suicide. Thus one in a hundred suicides are coupled with murder, and one in three murders are followed by suicide.

This report deals with persons who commit murder and then kill themselves, and describes the findings from an unselected sample of such cases. Although numerically insignificant in comparison with other categories of crime, such as theft, fraud or vandalism, these incidents have special importance for research. Murder itself is a relatively rare crime, especially in England, but it has rightly been considered a fit subject for close study, since extreme examples of uncontrolled aggression shed light on the factors responsible for many lesser forms of anti-social hostility and violence. And if the study of murder is important, the study of murder-suicide must also be important, for this constitutes a sizeable proportion of all murders in this country. Indeed, it is not generally appreciated that statistical

1

surveys of murder will yield appreciably different findings according to whether murder-suicide incidents, which have their own particular features, are included or not.

In their study of murder in England and Wales in the years 1952 to 1960 the Home Office researchers Gibson and Klein mentioned that 'in each year, about one-third of all suspects in cases finally recorded as murder committed suicide'.[1] In over half of murders known to have been committed by women suicide follows the crime.[2] For this reason a substantial proportion of murderers never come to trial. Such cases arouse little public attention, although they have considerable interest, especially from the psychiatric point of view. Dr Gavin Thurston, the West London coroner, has also drawn attention to this, remarking that in England and Wales in the year 1954, for example, 'the coroner completed the proceedings in over a third of all cases of murder', and further pointing out that the special characteristics of this class of case, often pitiful more than heinous, should be remembered when murder statistics are considered.[3]

The proportion of murderers who commit suicide appears to have remained fairly constant in England for many years. The late Sir Norwood East noted that: 'During the years 1929–32 inclusive there were known to the police 338 cases of murder of 393 persons aged over 1 year. In 131 cases, involving 165 victims, the murderer or suspect committed suicide.'[4]

Recent statistics of attempted suicides following murders have not been published, but going back to Norwood East again one reads that 'in a series of 182 persons convicted of murder, whose mental condition I examined, 41 attempted suicide in connection with the crime' and that 'of 537 admissions to Broadmoor during the last twenty years following charges of murder, 149 attempted suicide at the time of the crime'.[5] In a recent study of 40 murderers and 40 attempted murderers who were patients in Broadmoor, selected on account of symptoms of morbid jealousy, Dr R. R. Mowat noted that

[1] *Murder*, H.M.S.O. (London, 1961), p. 7
[2] ibid., Table 27, p. 26
[3] *Coroner's Practice* (London, 1958), p. 163
[4] *Medical Aspects of Crime* (London, 1936), p. 368
[5] ibid., p. 280

28·5% had attempted suicide following their crime, and that a quarter had made suicidal attempts prior to committing their crime.[1] In a recent and not yet published study of a consecutive and unselected series of 254 persons convicted of murder (or of manslaughter under Section 2 of the Homicide Act, 1957) or found guilty but insane, Dr B. A. O'Connell, a consultant psychiatrist at Broadmoor Hospital, found that 15% of the offenders had attempted suicide subsequent to the crime. Dividing the offenders into normal and mentally abnormal groups, he found the incidence of attempted suicide to be 11% and 21% respectively.[2] Evidently something like a half of murders in England are followed by the suicide or attempted suicide of the aggressor.

The mentally sick, especially those suffering from depressive psychosis (melancholia), have a particular liability to suicide. The fact that so many murders are linked with suicide could be argued to support the contention that most murders are committed in a state of madness, and that the true proportion of murderers who are 'insane' is even higher than appears from official criminal statistics, which naturally derive only from those who survive to come to trial. This argument, based upon high suicidal incidence among murderers, carries slender weight, since suicides arise from many causes unrelated to psychotic illness. Estimates of the proportion of recognizable psychotic persons among those who succeed in killing themselves vary according to the type of community studied, percentages ranging from 5 to 30 having been reported by different investigators.

The question of the incidence and type of psychotic disturbance among murder-suicide cases has practical as well as academic interest. If it should turn out that psychotic illness is the cause of most of these incidents, then improved methods of identifying and treating these potentially dangerous illnesses might achieve a substantial reduction in the murder rate. An important line of inquiry, therefore, is a close study of mental patients who commit murder-suicides with a view to discovering

[1] R. R. Mowat, *Morbid Jealousy and Murder* (at press, London, Tavistock Publications)
[2] B. A. O'Connell, 'Personal Communication,' 6 January 1963

special features or warning symptoms which might serve to avert some of these tragedies.

In England and Wales deaths by suicide are over ten times as frequent as deaths from murder and manslaughter combined. Suicide ends almost as many lives as traffic accidents, and although suicide is relatively more frequent in the aged it nevertheless represents a commoner cause of death in young adults than most of the well-known lethal diseases. With the decrease in infectious diseases and other scourges, suicide has become one of the most outstanding problems in public health. In so far as a study of murder-suicide cases throws some light on suicide in general, it may contribute something relevant to this problem.

At first sight, ordinary suicides seem to have nothing in common with murder-suicide incidents. The sick and lonely old person who decides life is not worth continuing, or the rejected and despondent lover who decides to renounce the struggle, can hardly be compared with an aggressive destroyer of an innocent victim. In his desire to remove the burden of his presence the suicide appears self-effacing, almost altruistic; in sacrificing another person's life to his own ends or passions the murderer appears selfish and ruthless. Two common theories of the likely motives in suicides following murder emphasize this contrast. On one view the subsequent suicide is a normal reaction of remorse and guilt following a crime committed un-thinkingly in the heat of passion. On another view, the suicide represents a form of escape when the murderer finds himself threatened with detection and punishment.

Other more subtle motivational theories have linked both murder and suicide. On one view the act of suicide, far from being a passive renunciation, constitutes a violent explosion of aggression which is directed against the self only because lack of opportunity or moral restraints prevent the killing of the person responsible for arousing the anger. A vast amount of psychological theorizing and research has gone into the elucidation of factors in the individual's constitution and personality development which decide whether his aggression tends to vent itself in open hostility against others or to turn inwards against himself in self-punishing feelings and acts. Theories of human aggression, and of the factors which stimulate it and determine its expression in either self-destructive or externally destructive forms, have very wide application in criminology, since almost all crimes can be interpreted as manifestations of outwardly directed aggression. Some psychologists suggest that reactions to stress and frustration take two main paths, the hitting back reactions, which produce rebellious and anti-social behaviour, and the self-criticizing and self-punishing reactions, which produce anxiety-neurosis and psycho-somatic illness. Such a viewpoint seems to carry the implication that a policy of vigorous suppression of rebelliousness, without attention to underlying social malaise, may merely result in increasing the incidence of neurosis. The interconnection between murder and suicide, although a highly specialized study, is of particular interest as a source of evidence on the nature of aggression, a topic of crucial importance to criminology.

Sociologists have interested themselves in the consistent differences between members of different communities and social classes in regard to the preponderance of outwardly or internally directed aggression. They have sought explanations for this in terms of varying cultural pressures whereby openly expressed aggression is more severely condemned and suppressed in some communities than in others. Statistics of incidence of homicide and suicide provide a favourite hunting ground for such theorists, since the demonstration of a reciprocal relationship between these two (homicide rates being high in communities with a low suicide rate and *vice versa*) lends support to the idea that communities can be characterized according to whether their members direct their aggression inwards or outwards.

A number of investigators who have concerned themselves with this type of theory have recognized the relevance of an examination of the nature of murder-suicide incidents. For instance, Porterfield, when reporting the results of a comparison of the homicide and suicide incidence in various American towns, remarked that 'of special importance would be a study of the extent to which persons who commit homicide kill themselves immediately after the homicidal act.'[1] Lithner,

[1] 'Indices of homicides and suicides by states and cities,' *Amer. Sociol. Review*, 1949

following an analysis of the relationships between murder-suicide and business cycles in Sweden, also suggested a study of cases of combined murder and suicide.[1]

On the theory that the typical suicide is a frustrated murderer, one would certainly expect some instances in which aggression spills over and, as it were, engulfs a second person. One might even predict on the theory the kind of circumstances in which this might be expected to occur. For example, in a community with a strong cultural prohibition against violence, in which people habitually respond to frustration by inward turned aggression, only very direct and personal provocation would produce external violence. A deserting or rejecting lover might supply sufficient provocation, but even then the anger would be turned against the self just as much as against the other person. Ruth Cavan described this kind of situation as follows:

> The person interprets his difficulty as sufficient to prohibit adjustment; he has, he believes, reached the end of the way, and suicide is a means of solution for him. But his happiness has been ruined or is prevented by some person. Before he kills himself he kills that person, in anger and revenge, or in jealousy and to prevent another from succeeding where he has failed.[2]

Another theory to explain the frequent combination of suicide and murder concerns the influence of psychotic depression. Sufferers from this illness account for most of the suicides that take place in mental hospitals. They become so convinced of the utter hopelessness of their misery that death becomes a happy escape. Sometimes, before committing suicide, they first kill their children or other members of the family. From the accounts given subsequently by patients who have been revived after such an occurrence the motives for the murder have been quite altruistic. Under the delusion of a future without hope, and the inevitability of catastrophe overtaking their nearest and dearest as well as themselves, they decide to kill in order to spare their loved ones suffering. This sequence of events, although fortunately infrequent in relation to the numbers of depressed

---

[1] 'Mord och ajalvmord,' *Nord T. Kriminalvidensk*, 1962
[2] *Suicide* (1928)

patients, nevertheless happens often enough to constitute one of the commonest forms of murder, and has long been recognized by psychiatrists and criminologists as an important factor in murder statistics.

The insane yet altruistically motivated suicidal murderer would seem to constitute a striking exception to the theory that suicides arise from hostile impulses only partially deflected inwards. Perhaps the psycho-pathology of murder-suicide runs in opposite directions in the sane and insane.

Search through criminological literature yields surprisingly little in the way of hard facts about murder-suicide incidents with which to compare these various theories. Individual case reports, illustrative of one particular theory, occur fairly frequently, but studies covering an unselected series of these incidents have been limited to the United States. Statistical information is available for some countries on the proportions of murders which are associated with suicide. This varies remarkably. R. W. McKenzie, in a study of murder records in New South Wales, found that the proportion of suicidal murderers was slightly smaller than the figures for England and Wales. Of 767 persons (616 male) considered by the police to be responsible for murders in the period 1933 to 1957, 21·6% (125 male and 41 female) killed themselves afterwards and a further 4% (17 male and 14 female) made suicidal attempts.[1] S. Siciliano surveyed all homicides in Denmark (as defined by Act 27 of the Danish Penal Code) over a period of 28 years. Excluding political killings and those committed by German occupying forces during the last war, he found 545 cases of homicide. Of the Danish killers (34·6% of them women) 42·2% killed themselves subsequently, and a further 9·6% made a serious suicidal attempt. The incidence was particularly high among the female offenders, 63·9% killing themselves and 16·1% making serious suicidal attempts.[2]

In contrast, murder followed by suicide is a relatively unusual sequence of events in the United States. Wolfgang reports that 'in Philadelphia, only about 4 out of every 100 who commit criminal homicide kill themselves', and quotes incidence figures

[1] Personal Communication (thesis)
[2] 'Resultati preliminari di un 'indagine sull 'Omicido in Danimarca,' *Scuola Positiva*, 1961

as low or even lower from samples taken in other parts of the United States.[1] In Wolfgang's own study of 621 homicidal offenders (512 male), 4% (22 male and 2 female) killed themselves. He does not quote corresponding figures for attempts, but T. C. N. Gibbens, in a study in New Jersey, found that 6% of a sample of offenders charged with homicide had attempted suicide unsuccessfully following the crime, although less than 4% of suspects had actually killed themselves.[2]

It follows from the figures given that a significant variation in sex distribution of murder-suicide offenders accompanies the variation in frequency of these cases. Thus in the United States the ratio of male to female is about 11 to 1, in Australia about 3 to 1, in England about 1·7 to 1, and in Denmark about 1 to 1.

These contrasts in incidence of murder followed by suicide become still more puzzling when one considers them against the background of homicide and suicide rates for the countries concerned. One might suppose that the proportion of murderers who kill themselves would vary directly with the suicide rate, being large in countries like Denmark which have a high frequency of suicide. The briefest glance at the figures, however, suffices to show that variations in suicide rate, substantial though they are, could not in themselves account for the enormous differences in the proportions of murders followed by suicide. Another possibility is that murder-suicide tragedies remain relatively constant, while other types of murder fluctuate from one country to another. Some such expectation would follow from the theory that murder-suicide incidents are predominantly the work of depressive psychotics, always assuming that manic depressive psychosis is of fairly constant incidence and presents a relatively constant risk of violence. Since murder in general is so much commoner in the United States than in England, the same absolute number of murder-suicide incidents would represent a much less significant section of American murder cases. The figures in Table 1 (although only very rough

[1] 'An Analysis of Homicide-Suicide,' *Journ. Clinical and Exptl. Psychopathology*, 1958. *Illinois Crime Survey*, 1929

[2] 'Sane and Insane Homicide,' *Journ. Criminal Law, Criminal and Police Science*, 1958

approximations on account of the difficulty of obtaining comparable definitions of criminal homicide) suggest that in fact the incidence of murder-suicides is far from constant, but they provide no clue to the source of the variation. As a consequence of the high American murder rate, the low proportion of 4% of criminal homicides still represents an incidence of homicide-suicide cases in excess of that of England and Wales. The number of ordinary suicides is also greater in the United States.

These contrasts have some relevance to the hypothesis that in communities where violence turns against the self rather than against others (thus producing high suicide to murder ratios) such homicides as do occur will be followed by suicide in a high proportion of cases. Table 1 sets out a rough comparison of the incidences of criminal homicide, homicide followed by suicide, and suicide, for four countries. In the two countries with very high suicide-murder ratios, England and Denmark, where suicides are respectively 30 times and 40 times commoner than homicides, the percentage of offenders who kill themselves is very high. In the United States, where suicide is not much more than twice as common than homicide, the percentage of suicidal murderers is small. In Australia the figures are in all respects intermediate. Thus, as far as they go, the figures support the hypothesis.

The first investigator to inquire into the circumstances of murder-suicide incidents was Ruth Cavan.[1] In a study of suicides in Chicago she found that, according to coroners' records for the year 1923, 18 individuals had killed or attempted to kill one or more persons before taking their own lives. To this group she added a further 21 unselected cases from other years. Her description of these 39 suicides preceded by murder constitutes the first case study of an unselected sample. Unfortunately she only occasionally gives precise figures, and she does not give the age or sex distribution of offenders, but she makes some very definite statements about the frequency of different types of incident. In flat contradiction of psychiatric expectations, she found that insane persons were rarely responsible for murder-suicide incidents. In the 1923 sample there was only one instance of an insane offender. He was an aggressive paranoid psychotic who shot his sister-in-law because he thought

[1] *Suicide*, op. cit.

she wanted to put him away. In this same period there had been 57 ordinary suicides committed by persons with definite evidence of insanity.

The most common type of murder-suicide in Cavan's observation was that committed in anger by an aggrieved person who decides to kill the person responsible for his suffering as well as himself. She cites as typical the case of a young man who had courted a woman for a long time and then had been told he was too young and didn't have enough money to marry. He shot her and himself, leaving behind a suicide note wishing his friends to be spared 'from the hell that I have gone through'. The grievance was not always associated with a love affair. In another case a workman was sacked for disobeying his foreman. He said nothing to his wife about it, but returned to his place of work the following day to shoot the foreman and kill himself.

Cavan also noted some examples of superficially altruistic motivation, in which the suicide kills someone because he believes them to be completely dependent upon him and liable to suffer without his continued protection. Such appeared to be the attitude of the mother who killed her children and herself after her husband had deserted her for another woman and left her without money. In another case a sick mother killed her two youngest children leaving behind a note explaining that she was sorry for them and was taking them with her.

In some of the cases reported by Cavan (unfortunately she does not specify what proportion of her sample) the suicide follows a considerable time after the murder, usually as a result of detection and fear of punishment and public disgrace. 'Such a suicide is not different from any suicide or attempted suicide by a criminal whose morale has been destroyed by long hours of official questioning. . . . Undetected, the murderer would have lived on.'

A smaller sample of 24 murder-suicides has been reported in greater detail by Wolfgang.[1] These were taken from a total group of 621 offenders recorded by the police as having been responsible for the criminal homicide of 588 victims in Philadelphia in 1948–52. In only 3 cases out of the 24 did the suicide take place after the offender had been arrested and taken to prison, but Wolfgang concurs with Cavan's view that, when

[1] 'An Analysis of Homicide and Suicide,' op. cit.

such a lapse of time does occur, remorse or fear is the probable motive for the suicide.

Wolfgang considered only 3, that is 12·5%, of his murder-suicide offenders to be insane,[1] but this has to be taken in conjunction with the small number of murderers found insane by the Courts in U.S.A. In Wolfgang's Philadelphia sample of homicides, out of 597 tried, only 17, that is 2·8%, were declared insane.

Nearly all Wolfgang's murder-suicide cases consisted of the killing of a spouse or lover. Of the 26 victims, 10 were wives killed by their husbands, 6 were women killed by their lovers, one was a husband killed by his wife, and one was a lover killed by his mistress. Of the remaining 8 victims, all but one were relatives of the offenders. The predominant pattern of these cases was as described by Cavan, namely, a history of personal friction between victim and offender culminating in a final outburst of violence. Among the cases quoted as typical was a husband who lost his temper when his wife nagged him for staying out all night, and drew a gun, shooting the wife and himself in the presence of their 14-year-old daughter. In another example, an estranged husband tried to persuade his wife to return. When she refused he shot her and then ran from the house and drowned himself. Wolfgang mentions only one instance of child killing, described as 'a case where no motive was discovered', in which a woman of 48 gassed her 3-year-old son and herself, both being found dead when the husband returned from work.

[1] ibid., ii, p. 312

II

Method of Study

THE purpose of the present inquiry was to investigate, primarily by means of a survey of documentary records, the situations and types of individuals involved in murder-suicide crimes in England. The main sample used for the study consisted of an unselected series of 78 incidents in which a murder of one or more victims was followed by the suicide of the offender. The cases were identified from police records. A search through the 'murder book' at the Criminal Record Office, Scotland Yard, which lists all cases initially recorded by the police as crimes of murder, produced a total of 60 murder-suicide incidents in the London Metropolitan Police District during the years 1954 to 1961. A similar inquiry at Police Headquarters in three Home Counties yielded a further 18 cases during the same 8-year period. The Home Office Research Unit kindly checked the names against the homicide returns and found the list correct and complete. Within the time span and area specified, the sample included every known instance in which a murder suspect killed himself before being brought to trial. The survey was centred on the London area on account of the convenient access to a substantial number of well-documented cases. There is no reason to suppose the sample unrepresentative of murder-suicide in other parts of the country, and in fact it comprised approximately one-quarter of the total number occurring in the whole of England and Wales.

Of this main sample of 78 suicidal offenders, all but one killed themselves before arrest, and consequently they appear in the annual criminal statistics of murder in the category of homicide suspects known to the police but not charged. The solitary exception was a young man who killed himself in prison while awaiting trial. The question arises whether the method of selection excluded any offenders who may have committed suicide at a later stage, that is while awaiting execution or while serving a term of imprisonment. Actually, the suicide of a convicted murderer in prison is an uncommon event in England, only two instances occurring in a period of 7 years. The Prison Commissioners kindly helped by verifying that no one found guilty of murder within the times and areas covered by this survey had killed himself while a convicted prisoner.

In every case, the appropriate police authorities gave access to the file which recorded their investigations, and in nearly all cases the coroners who had carried out inquests on the victims allowed access to their records also. (As a general rule, however, almost all the information in the coroners' files was also on record in the police files.) In addition to police and coroners' records, further reports were sought whenever possible from family doctors, probation officers, social workers and others professionally concerned. Whenever the murderer or victim was known to have been treated in a mental hospital, permission to study the relevant medical records was requested. Altogether, some 90 individuals or organizations were written to, and 43 informants were individually interviewed by an assistant qualified in sociological research. For ethical reasons relatives or others personally involved in the tragedies were not approached. There were available finally, in addition to post-mortem findings, 76 medical reports, including 25 from psychiatrists.

A sample of this size was sufficient for detailed case studies, but for the purpose of making further statistical comparisons an extended list was prepared of a further 70 cases, consisting of all murder-suicide incidents in the Metropolitan Police District, during the years 1946 to 1962 inclusive, that had not already been included in the main sample. From the data on file at Scotland Yard, basic information about this supplementary sample (such as the age, sex, civil state and relationships between offender and victim, the time, place and method of killing) was transferred to a prepared schedule and used for statistical tabulations.

The total sample of 148 offenders who committed both murder and suicide was compared with a sample of 148 murder incidents in which the offenders had been found insane, or had been convicted of murder, or (since the Homicide Act, 1957) of murder reduced to manslaughter by virtue of 'diminished responsibility'. These were unselected cases in the Metropolitan Police District or Home Counties taken from the same years as the murder-suicide cases. As far as possible each murder-suicide case was matched by the chronologically nearest murder case recorded in the 'murder book' at Scotland Yard. Without this additional data collection on convicted murderers, it would have been impossible to verify generalizations about the difference between ordinary murder and murder-suicide, for the amount of published information on either group is limited in the extreme.

From now on the 78 cases studied in detail are called the *main sample* of murder-suicides, the extra 70 cases added to provide sufficient numbers for statistical comparison comprise the *supplementary sample*, and the total collection is referred to simply as the *murder-suicide sample*. The comparative group of 148 offenders charged with murder is called the *murder sample*. Unless otherwise stated the examples cited in the text (and numbered 1 to 78) are drawn from the main sample, and a list of these, giving the page references where they occur, is set out in the Appendix. Cases from the murder sample are given, reference numbers commencing at 500.

Since the findings of the survey are described and discussed from several different points of view, it may avoid some confusion to outline the scheme of presentation adopted. First of all, in Chapter III, the criteria for defining murder-suicide are given, and examples of borderline cases of accident and suicide pact are mentioned to illustrate the range of incidents included. Next, in Chapter IV, the total murder-suicide sample and the comparative sample of murders brought to trial are contrasted on a number of basic points, such as the offenders' age, sex, social class, relationship to victim, previous criminal history, and mental state, the time and place of the crimes, and the apparent motives. The points of contrast that emerge are compared with those reported in some previous studies in America and Denmark.

In Chapters V and VI, actual cases from the main murder-suicide sample are individually described, in which the killings were committed by persons who appear, at least superficially, to be sane. Chapter V deals with the crimes of the sane and non-criminal offenders, and Chapter VI describes the crimes of those with previous convictions. Chapter VII continues the case descriptions, but deals with the murder-suicides by 'insane' or seriously abnormal offenders, commencing with some statistics of incidence, and then proceeding to accounts of the chief abnormalities encountered, namely depressive illness, schizophrenia, morbid jealousy, aggressive psychopathy and severe neurotic instability. The chapter closes with some account of how the incidence and distribution of abnormalities among these murder-suicide offenders compares with what has been reported of insane murderers brought to trial.

Since depressive illness was so frequent among the murder-suicide offenders, Chapter VIII is devoted to an account of the psychological processes which lead some melancholics to commit these crimes. For this purpose, psychiatric literature on the topic, as well as the results of the present survey, are considered, and special attention is paid to the important question of how to identify the homicidally dangerous patients. In Chapter IX, the psychology of murder-suicide by sane persons is similarly discussed. For this purpose, the theory that murder and suicide constitute alternative forms of aggression is considered at some length, with particular reference to the aggressive elements in ordinary suicidal behaviour. This leads to an analysis of the balance of motives, hostile or self-destructive, as they appeared in the murder-suicide sample. Finally, in Chapter X, the social factors that may influence the incidence of murder combined with suicide are discussed, and the theories of Durkheim and later sociologists in this regard are described. Chapter XI summarizes the main findings.

III

The Borderline of Murder

STRICTLY speaking, murder suspects who kill themselves are not precisely comparable with those who go to trial. They are identified on police evidence only, and no opportunity occurs for the due processes of law to produce any acquittals or reductions of the charge to one of a lesser crime, such as manslaughter or infanticide. Thus, had these suspects survived, a few of them would very likely have been removed from the class of murder.

The following example shows how this may come about. In this case a killer had to be omitted from the series because he delayed his suicide until after being taken into custody, by which time the charge against him was reduced from murder to manslaughter. Had he killed himself more promptly, while he was still labelled a murderer, he would have been one of the sample:

Case 282
A small but tough young man, with an urge to assert himself with his fists, had had two previous convictions, one for assault occasioning actual bodily harm. Together with some friends, all of whom had been drinking, he followed an elderly bookmaker to his home, and robbed him. In the struggle the victim fell, fracturing his thigh bone, as a result of which he ultimately died in hospital from hypostatic pneumonia, a well-known complication of enforced confinement to bed. A few days after his conviction for manslaughter, the young man hanged himself in his prison cell.

Incidentally, the association of delayed suicide with a typically criminal offender motivated, at least in part, by desire to escape punishment occurs again in one or two cases in the main sample.

An opposite effect, that is a reduction in the apparent

number of murders, may result occasionally from homicides being attributed to suicide pacts. When all the participants in a family tragedy are found dead, the need for exhaustive inquiries seems not particularly pressing, and if appearances suggest that they all died by their own hand, the possibility of murder may not be pursued too actively. In the following pages several examples are quoted of deaths attributed to accident or suicide which occurred in circumstances rather similar to those of some of the cases in the sample of murderers.

In practice these considerations arise in a few cases only, for the circumstances usually indicate beyond doubt whether a deliberate murder has occurred. The decision as to how doubtful cases should be classified could hardly have much statistical significance, and would certainly not invalidate any of the comparisons and trends noted in subsequent sections of this report, but the existence of these cases raises some interesting issues, and for this reason deserves mention.

The decision as to how a case should be recorded by the Home Office in the criminal statistics is based on a review of the evidence submitted by the police in their homicide returns. In the main series, all 78 incidents were finally included in the criminal statistics as murders known to the police. The conclusion arrived at by the police that a victim has been murdered, and their identification of the suspect, need not necessarily coincide with the finding of the jury at the inquest, and in fact an 'open' verdict was returned in one of the 78 cases. In another instance, in which the possibility of accidental death was raised, the jury deliberated for half an hour before finally returning a verdict of murder. These verdicts do not influence the criminal statistics, which are compiled independently.

In 3 out of the 78 incidents in the main sample, the sole deceased victim was a baby under one year old killed by the mother. Had these women come to trial they would normally have been convicted under the Infanticide Act, 1929, which allows of much lesser penalties than murder. One of these women, however, also committed attempted murder, in that she attacked an older child as well, but not fatally. No cases of child destruction (that is killing of a baby before it has an existence independent of the mother) were encountered in the series, and in fact a negligibly small number are recorded annually.

In the following anomalous case, a man killed himself with gas, and as a result of an unfortunate leakage unintentionally killed one of his family. This was recorded by the police as an accidental death, and was not included in the homicide returns, although had the killer survived on this occasion, he would presumably have been charged with murder, under the old law of transferred malice.[1] This, however, has probably been changed by the Suicide Act, 1961. The coroner's verdict on the case was 'unlawful killing'.

Case 279
Serious marital friction existed as a result of a husband's addiction to alcohol, which led him to incur debts and to commit various frauds in vain attempts at repayment. The wife several times threatened suicide and said she would take her child with her. Knowing that his frauds were about to be exposed, and being to some extent intoxicated, the husband went downstairs during the night and gassed himself in the kitchen. Although the door was closed, a draught carried the gas upstairs and killed the sleeping child

Had this case formed part of the sample, it would have added to the small number of cases in which the main stress consisted of the threatened exposure of offences. In general, members of the predatory criminal classes regard prosecutions as a nuisance rather than a shameful degradation warranting suicide, but in this case, as in similar cases in the sample, the offender was not an habitual criminal and had no record of previous convictions.

In the instance just quoted, circumstantial evidence of accident rather than design was accepted by the police, but in another case officially recorded as murder, and therefore included in the main sample, the circumstances could have been interpreted on the theory of accident:

Case 59
A young man was visited one morning by his girl-friend of long standing. Her parents disapproved, because he had recently been

---

[1] Kenny, *Outlines of Criminal Law* 18th Ed. (Cambridge, 1962), p. 175. Also, R. *v.* Spence (1957), 41 Criminal Appeal Reports, 80

going about with a delinquent gang, and there was a possibility she had come to tell him she intended to break off their friendship. He had a gun in the room and shot her at close range, immediately afterwards rushing about in extreme distress shouting for a doctor. He appeared grief-stricken when told she had died, and repeated several times that he did not want to live. He made a statement to the effect that he had been showing off the gun playfully and had not intended to fire it. Before this defence could be tested, he killed himself.

In the next instance from the main sample the coroner's jury took a long time to decide before reaching the verdict of murder. In fact, in his address to the jury, the coroner explained that the possibility of accidental death was not ruled out, although he pointed out the various features which seemed to indicate otherwise. Some years later a High Court judge, considering the claims of the estate of the supposed murderer, commented that there were other possibilities just as consistent with the circumstances as felonious killing. He decided that no murder had occurred, and ruled that the estate was entitled to benefit from the 'victim's' will:

Case 38
An elderly and rather wealthy spinster, sharing a house with her aged mother, lived in extreme social isolation, in drab dilapidated surroundings, enjoying only the barest necessities. For a year or more she had become increasingly anxious about her health. She suffered from arthritis only, but she had an unfounded idea she was going blind, or becoming a helpless cripple, and frequently expressed concern about what would happen to the old mother if she were to die. Her doctor did his best to reassure her, but she had very rigid ideas, could not take advice, and became increasingly miserable and querulant.
    The two women were found one afternoon dead from gas poisoning, the old mother sitting at the kitchen table, which was laid for tea, the daughter lying near the gas cooker, with some taps half on but not lit. Some dusters were stuffed into the ventilator above the cooker, but no other indications of suicidal preparations were evident, and a filled kettle and saucepan of milk rested in normal positions on the top of the cooker.

Case 38, quoted above, could equally well serve as an example of a possible suicide pact, supposing that the old mother, influenced by her daughter's agitation and depression, had agreed to the turning on of the gas. Two types of pact may occur. In the commoner variety, those concerned decide they wish to die, and thereafter act independently, each taking his own life, in which case inquest verdicts of suicide will be returned on all parties. Occasionally, however, a death pact is made in which one person asks or consents that the other should first kill him and then commit suicide. From a psychological standpoint these still remain suicide pacts, but since one person has taken action to kill the other this will be recorded as murder. One clear example of this type occurred in the present sample (Case 64) as well as several others (e.g. Case 35), in which the victim may possibly have been willing to die, although the balance of evidence suggested otherwise.

Suicide pacts occur less frequently than murder followed by suicide. In a study of simultaneous deaths by interconnected suicide Professor John Cohen found 60 instances in England and Wales over the 4-year period from 1955 to 1958.[1] This represents an incidence of the order of two-fifths that of the suicide-homicide cases. Since the members of most suicide pacts die in circumstances indicating plainly that each killed himself, it follows that the indeterminate cases are statistically unimportant. The elimination from the homicide returns of all doubtful cases, and of all cases of killings by consent, would make but little difference to the national murder rate. However, from the point of view of the individual, and especially in the eyes of surviving relatives the decision in such matters may cause concern, and may occasionally have a material influence on the disposal of property, since a murderer may not benefit from or pass on to his heirs the proceeds of his victim's estate. Furthermore, to the plain man it may seem unjustified that any cases so far removed from ordinary ideas of what constitutes murder as some of the examples quoted here should be used to swell the number of officially recorded murders.

The legal position of the survivors of suicide pacts now depends upon two statutes, the Homicide Act of 1957, and the Suicide Act of 1961. The Homicide Act applies to the homicide-suicide pact in which the victim consents to be killed on the understanding that the killer will commit suicide. A person

[1] 'A Study of Suicide Pacts,' *Medico-Legal Journal*, 1961

who has killed in the furtherance of a genuine homicide-suicide pact is no longer regarded as having committed murder, but he is punishable for manslaughter if he should survive. The Suicide Act applies to the pact of double suicide and makes a survivor, by virtue of being an accomplice in another person's suicide, liable to prosecution for a special offence punishable with up to fourteen years' imprisonment. The Act refers to a person who aids, abets, counsels or procures the suicide or attempted suicide of another. In practice, survivors of double suicides are not actually prosecuted, presumably because the definition of the offence implies more than passive acquiesence in the other person's death. Where both members of a pact die, the opportunity to put these defences forward does not occur, since no trial takes place. At inquests, if one person has deliberately killed another, the verdict has to be murder unless the circumstances are so unclear as to allow the deceased the benefit of the doubt, in which case open verdicts or verdicts of suicide may be returned. The harshness of the finding may be further reduced by the addition of a rider such as 'while the balance of the mind was disturbed' to the verdict on the suicide of a person who has been named as a killer. The use of this formula, however, is a matter of sentiment rather than of law, since the official business of the inquest nowadays is not to determine state of mind, but to ascertain how death came about. Furthermore, it is outside the power of the coroner and his jury to pronounce upon the sanity or otherwise of a person at the time of committing a felonious homicide.[1]

The sometimes unfortunate consequences of the present law governing inquests in these kinds of tragedies has recently received adverse criticism. Mr Justice Ungoed-Thomas, hearing a case arising out of the disputed will of a husband who had been found dead from coal gas poisoning, remarked that the law bearing upon such a case was clumsy, crude and somewhat uncivilized. The husband, a helpless invalid, had been killed by a devoted wife, who was herself suffering from exhaustion and depression, and had spoken of suicide and fears of who would look after her husband if she died first. The couple were found in a gas-filled kitchen with doors and windows fastened, all the gas taps turned on, and mats placed

---

[1] See J. Jervis, *The Office and Duties of Coroners* (London, 1957), pp. 180, 217.

against the bottom of the door. There was no evidence of insanity within the legal meaning of that term, and although this was clearly a case for compassion rather than condemnation his Lordship found he could come to no other conclusion than that the wife had feloniously killed her husband and that the wife's estate could not benefit from the husband's will.[1] Some improvement in this matter could be achieved if coroners were allowed at least to put the issues of diminished responsibility or infanticide or homicide pacts to the inquest juries in cases in which these defences could have applied at a criminal trial. Verdicts of murder seem particularly inappropriate to cases of death pacts.

The following case, taken from the main sample of murder-suicides, was a clear instance of a death pact in which husband and wife resolved to die together – an unqualified verdict of murder by the husband had to be returned at the inquest since he had taken the initiative in the killing:

Case 64
An unhappy couple with a long history of marital disputes were faced with an impossible demand to replace some money the husband had obtained illegally some time ago. The wife had been under treatment for years for symptoms of hysteria and depression, and she had in fact made one suicidal attempt previously.

The husband shot his wife and then himself. They left behind joint letters, explaining their intentions, together with clear instructions on business matters and bequests. Their activities immediately beforehand left no room for doubt that both anticipated suicide and made orderly arrangements for it.

The above example illustrates well some of the points about suicide pacts noted by Cohen. He found they conformed to a pattern of their own which differed from most suicides and most suicide-homicides. Except for the rare possibility of infectitious madness, *folie à deux*, the need for co-operative planning in suicide pacts virtually excluded psychotic cases in which baseless delusions lead to senseless sacrifices of life. From his sixty instances of double suicide Cohen found two cases in which the first suicide precipitated the second. In all other cases the deaths resulted from pacts in which two people

[1] *The Times*, 7 February 1964

resolved to end their lives at the same time. The typical suicide pact involved ageing married couples in truly sad circumstances, failing health and increasing isolation being common complaints. They plan their deaths carefully, so that one rarely survives the other, and they make careful arrangements on financial and other matters so as not to cause complications to others.

In Cohen's series 70% of the deceased were over fifty (which is not different from suicides in general), but 70% were married couples (whereas the single, widowed or separated account for a half of ordinary suicides).[1] Cohen noted that certain features common among ordinary suicides, for instance the element of outward aggression (as revealed in spiteful recriminations in suicide notes or the use of modes of death that inconvenience or endanger others) or the element of appeal for help (as revealed in contrived situations involving a chance of rescue) were rare in suicide pacts.

In two other instances in the main murder-suicide sample the circumstances left scope for interpretation in terms of a possible suicide pact, but in neither case was the evidence conclusive:

Case 2
A criminal couple, wanted by the police and temporarily destitute, deposited various letters addressed to relatives indicating that they intended to end their lives and making requests regarding financial matters. Soon after they were found lying dead together in a hotel bedroom, having taken poison. Medical evidence suggested that the man killed himself a day later than the woman, and some unexplained bruises inflicted on her just before death gave rise to the suggestion that she had not carried out her resolve of her own, unaided volition.

In the following instance, some co-operation from the two victims seems probable, although they were recorded as having been murdered:

Case 70
A married woman and her 2 teen-age daughters were found dead in their beds with the gas taps fully on. The coroner directed the

---

[1] See Peter Sainsbury, *Suicide in London* (London, 1955) Table 13 C, p. 66.

jury that there was no direct evidence as to who turned them on, and accordingly open verdicts were returned at the inquest on all 3 persons.

Circumstantial evidence supported the police view that the mother was responsible. She was an aggressive, quarrelsome woman who completely dominated her children and had recently driven away her husband by constant nagging. His refusal to return unless she accepted the psychiatric help she had hitherto refused probably precipitated her desperate act. Some time ago, during one of the many marital rows, she had threatened to gas herself.

As the above illustrations show, some suicide pacts may be included in the statistics of murder on somewhat dubious evidence. On the other hand, some actual murders may be excluded from the statistics because they look like genuine suicide pacts. In the following example, kindly drawn to our attention by the coroner, the case was rightly regarded by both police and jury as a triple suicide, although the murder theory could not be completely disproved:

Case 281
Husband, wife and husband's mistress were found dead together, having swallowed aspirin and turned on the gas. Medical evidence suggested that the mistress had waited for the aspirin to take effect with the other two before taking some herself and turning on the gas. Suicide notes were found written by the husband and the mistress.

Since the wife must have swallowed the aspirin with her husband, suspicion that she was an unwilling party to the pact was dispelled. Despite the evidence as to who turned on the gas, it was accepted that all three were responsible for their own deaths, and verdicts of suicide were returned on each one.

Limiting the survey to a small, strictly defined sample of murders meant cutting across some natural psychological groupings and may even have given a misleading impression that the size of the social problem is smaller than is in fact the case. Reference has just been made to doubtful suicide pacts, not counted as homicides, which were nevertheless similar to some cases included in the sample. Larger in number are instances of intended murder-suicide in which either the assaulted victim or the would-be suicide, or both, are rescued and revived. Some indication of the chances of survival is given by the fact that in the present sample, out of 26 attempts to kill more than one person, in 8 instances one or more of the victims survived. In the following example, given to us by the police, the two victims both survived, and so the case had to be excluded, although in other respects the circumstances were identical with those of many cases in the sample:

Case 280
A hard-working ambitious man, free from criminal convictions, but subject to violent tempers, in which he occasionally hit out at members of his family, was apparently devoted to his wife and children. His wife, however, complained that he sometimes illtreated her, and he apparently held against her the fact that their marriage was 'forced' by her pregnancy when they were very young.

The wife had a brief adulterous affair, and when the man concerned decided it must cease she gassed herself. The following day, still acutely distressed by her death, the husband first scribbled a note about the disposition of his possessions and then took poison, at the same time giving some to his 2 children, telling them that they were going to join their mother. When they would not swallow the poison, he attempted to stab them to death. As he lay dying he said to a would-be rescuer 'go away, I want to be with my wife'.

In this example, the crime itself, notwithstanding its brutality, was primarily an extended suicide, based on the intention of uniting the family in death, and included the killing of the family's pet animal.

An attempt at suicide may fail from lack of determination, due perhaps to some ambivalence of motivation. Attempted suicides are six times as frequent as completed suicides, and research suggests that they often represent a desperate call for help rather than a settled wish to die.[1] Suicidal acts following murder, however, are usually serious, and the majority end in death. Under these circumstances one might expect to find an unusually high proportion of single-minded and determined attempts at self destruction. In the following example, for

---

[1] E. Stengel and N. G. Cook, *Attempted Suicide* (London, 1958)

instance, survival appeared to be fortuitous and unintended, and the background to the tragedy was very similar to that of many of the depressive women in the sample of completed suicides:

Case 283

A young mother was treated in hospital for a depressive illness. Three months later she had a relapse under the influence of which she strangled her infant daughter. Leaving the child's body in bed, she went out and attempted suicide by jumping in front of a train. She explained later that she loved her daughter very much and had wished to spare the child the agonies of worry she had been through herself. She had expected to end her own life as well, and when rescued she said she would still like to take her life if she got the chance to do so. She was charged with murder, found unfit to plead, and committed to Broadmoor.

It should be clear from this discussion that cases of murders known to the police in which the suspect kills himself before being charged are not always so clear-cut and easily decided as one might at first sight suppose. The absence of a formal trial in such cases may result in some actual crimes being recorded as double suicides, but on the whole the effect is more likely to be an exaggeration of the statistics of murder, due to the inclusion of cases that might have been acquitted or reduced in the gravity of the charge had they come to Court.

IV

Murder and Murder-Suicide Compared

THE total sample of 148 incidents of murder followed by suicide was compared with a sample of 148 murder incidents in which the offenders were brought to Court on a murder charge and not acquitted. Except for two cases in which the offenders were finally sentenced for manslaughter owing to mitigating circumstances, all of them were either convicted of murder or 'diminished responsibility' manslaughter, or else found insane or unfit to plead. This murder sample was taken from the same area (130 cases from London, 18 from the Home Counties) and the same years as the murder-suicide sample and was thus more directly comparable than the national sample of all murders in England and Wales reported in the Home Office study by Gibson and Klein.[1] Nevertheless reference will be made to this national sample where occasion arises. In connection with the murder sample, no attempt was made to follow up the cases or to discover more about them than was on record in the files at Scotland Yard.

It has been pointed out very forcibly by Morris and Blom-Cooper that, 'In this country murder is overwhelmingly a domestic crime in which men kill their wives, mistresses and children, and women kill their children.'[2] Such violence is usually associated either with gross mental illness or with a long history of domestic discord or both. Murders of strangers committed by habitual criminals in the furtherance of theft (e.g. killing of night watchmen, police or others who try to prevent burglary, or way-laying and killing persons for the sake of robbing them) is relatively infrequent. The most obvious contrast between the murder and murder-suicide

---

[1] *Murder*, op. cit.
[2] *A Calendar of Murder* (London, 1964), p. 280

samples was found to be in the respective proportions of domestic and predatory crimes. In the murder sample, predatory crimes still constituted a minority, but they were considerably more frequent than in the murder-suicide sample.

The overwhelmingly domestic nature of murder-suicide showed up in almost every comparison made, but particularly in the high proportion of women offenders and child victims. The total sample of 148 murder-suicide offenders included 53 mothers who killed their children under 16, 62 men who killed their wives or girl-friends, 15 men who killed their children and in some instances their wives as well, and 3 women who killed a husband or lover. All 82 women victims were killed by men, with the exception of one killed by her mother and one by her daughter. Sixty-five women were killed by a husband or lover. Nearly all the murders followed by suicide took place in the home, and there were no instances of killings in the furtherance of theft or in the course of gang fights.

The 148 offenders in the total murder-suicide sample had taken the lives of 187 victims (an average of 1·26 victims for each offender), and 91 of these victims, almost half, were children under 16 years of age. In the main sample of 78 murder-suicide offenders, it was noted that in addition to the 106 victims who died there were a further 14 victims who survived attempts to murder them. The tendency for suicidal murderers to kill or try to kill more than one person is not peculiar to this study. The average number of deceased victims for each murder suspect who committed suicide was 1·36 in the Gibson and Klein survey, which covered the whole of England and Wales over the years 1952 to 1960.

In the murder-suicide sample, where there were multiple victims they were nearly always members of the offender's family, most frequently his own children. All the child victims under 16 were killed by their own parents. The sexes were represented more or less equally among these child victims (49 girls and 42 boys), but among the adult victims women were proportionately more numerous (82 women compared with only 14 men). This difference was due to the fact that most of the male offenders killed their women folk (wives or mistresses) and less often their children, whereas most of the female offenders killed their own children, boys and girls indiscriminately. In view of the traditional belief that women are peculiarly liable to kill their children during the puerperium, or before they have fully recovered from the effects of child-birth, it is relevant to notice that victims in their first year of life were not more numerous than victims in their later years of infancy. Of the 45 infant victims under 5 years of age, only 11 were babies of less than 12 months.

The murder-suicide sample contained no instance of offenders acting together as accomplices in murder. In contrast, the 148 incidents in the murder sample included 5 in which accomplices were convicted, and 7 in which 2 or more victims died. In total, the murder sample involved exactly equal numbers of offenders and victims, 156 of each.

These contrasts may now be considered in greater detail with reference to specific points.

Age and Sex of Offenders and Victims

The age and sex distribution of both offenders and victims differed markedly between the two samples (see Tables 2, 3 and 4). In the murder-suicide sample, 60 of the 148 offenders were women, that is 40·5%; in the murder sample only 11·5% of the offenders were women. In the total murder-suicide sample 48·7% of the victims were children under 16 years of age, compared with only 18% of child victims of murder. These differences clearly reflected the high proportion of mother-child killings among murder-suicides. In both samples the child victims were more or less equally divided between girls and boys, whereas women constituted the majority of adult victims. In the murder sample, however, males were relatively com-moner among the adult victims (33·6% as against 14·6% of males among the adult victims of murder-suicide), and also young male offenders were distinctly commoner (48·5% under 30 compared with 18·2% under 30 in the murder-suicide sample). These differences were associated with the presence in the murder sample of a group of young male criminals who were hardly represented at all in the murder-suicide sample. In the matter of age, the female murder-suicide offenders ran counter to the general trend in that they tended to be younger rather than older in comparison with women murderers brought to trial. This point will be considered in more detail later in connection with the actual circumstances of murder-suicide tragedies. The difference is undoubtedly due to the fact that young mothers killing their young children are especially frequent among English murder-suicides.

Although the ratio of men to women among the murder-suicide offenders was so much smaller than that which is found among ordinary murderers, it was in fact similar to what would be expected of a sample of ordinary suicides. The annual suicide rates for persons aged 15 or over in London and S.E. England are 20 per 100,000 for males and 13 for females, according to the Registrar-General's Statistical Review, 1960 (Table 21). Allowing for the slightly unequal distribution of men and women in the population, this works out at a male to female ratio of 4 to 3 for suicides compared with 4·4 to 3 in the murder-suicide sample.

The age distribution of the murder-suicide offenders, compared with that of suicides in England and Wales, as given by the World Health Organization (1961) is shown in Table 5. The offenders were in fact a younger group than the suicides, particularly so in the case of the females. The murder-suicide offenders were thus somewhere in between the younger age range typical of murderers and the older age range typical of suicides.

Relationship of Victims to Offenders

Scrutiny of the relationships between victims and offenders helps to clarify the implications of the age and sex differences already noted. Table 6 sets out the relationships of killers to their victims in the two samples. The most striking difference lay in the substantial proportion of offenders in the murder sample, amounting to nearly a half of the male murderers, who killed victims who were not related to them. In contrast, in the murder-suicide sample, only a quite small proportion of male offenders, less than 7%, murdered persons outside their family circle. As a corollary to this, the proportion of wife slayings by the men in the murder sample was relatively small, only 19% compared with 45% in the murder-suicide sample. There was also a comparatively small number of killings of children by their parents in the murder sample, which in turn was largely due to the comparatively small number of women offenders.

Mode of Death

Comparing the manner in which the victims in the two samples met their deaths[1] it appears that the murder-suicide offenders more frequently used gas poisoning than did the ordinary murderers. The difference was by no means accounted for by the high proportions of child victims and female offenders in the total murder-suicide sample. Whereas 87% of the child victims of murder-suicide died from coal gas, only 21% of the child victims of ordinary murder died in this manner. Of the adult victims in the murder sample, only one out of a total of 128 died from coal gas, compared with 12·6% of the adult victims of murder-suicide.

Apart from the advantage of simplicity in choosing the same method for killing as for subsequent suicide, some of the murder-suicide offenders probably used gas because they were actuated by motives of mercy – either rational or deluded – and this method appeared less cruel than cruder forms of violence. Whether killed by their mother or their father, very few of the child victims of murder-suicide died from stabbing, battering or strangling, whereas the majority of the child victims of ordinary murders died from such attacks.

In point of fact, in the total murder-suicide cases, the 60 women offenders mostly used gas and all killed both themselves and their victims by the same method, with the solitary exception of one mad woman (Case 77) who killed her husband with a chopper and then hanged herself. The 88 men used more varied methods. Only 11 killed both themselves and their victims with gas, although a further 18 used gas to kill themselves after a murder committed by some other method.

Death by shooting was markedly commoner among the victims of murder-suicide. Since shooting involves some degree of preparation, in the obtaining of a weapon and ammunition, this difference may possibly reflect the fact that some murder-suicide offenders acted after considerable deliberation and gave themselves time to select a swift and sure method. Among ordinary murders, robbery at gun point and gang warfare still comprise a very small minority of cases, insufficient to bring the percentage of victims of shooting to anywhere near the figure of the murder-suicide sample.

[1] See Table 7.

Marital and Social Status

In terms of social background the murder-suicide offenders were in no way remarkable. They came from all classes of society, most of them being respectable persons, living in conventional family groups, and free from criminal associations. Among the group of tried murderers, however, individuals of the lowest social class, and individuals poorly integrated into either the material or moral standards of the normal community, were considerably over-represented. This difference, which was fairly evident from reading police descriptions of the antecedents of the offenders, received some objective confirmation by comparisons of the distribution of occupations and marital status, the results of which appear in Tables 8 and 9.

Table 8 shows the classification of offenders according to civil status. In a few instances, the classification did not coincide with actual life circumstances. One woman in the murder-suicide sample, counted as a single person, had been living in stable cohabitation for 26 years, and another, counted as married, was in practice virtually separated, since she was staying with her husband's parents and would not let her husband approach her. However, such difficulties are inevitable in a simple classification, and they were not sufficiently numerous to affect the general picture.

In both the murder and the murder-suicide samples very few of the women offenders were single, indeed the proportion was much smaller than one would expect in a random sample of the adult population. (The actual distribution by marital status of men and women in Greater London, as given by the 1951 Census, is also shown in the Table.) This under-representation of single women is a natural consequence of the fact that murders by females, whether or not they commit suicide afterwards, mostly consist of the killing of their own children by married women.

The most interesting contrast was of the male offenders, who, of course, included the great majority of what might be called the 'criminal types'. In both samples, there was an extreme excess of separated and divorced persons compared with the normal population, doubtless a reflection of the very high incidence of mental instability in both groups of offenders. In the murder sample, however, there was also a considerable excess of unmarried male offenders. This excess appeared to be closely associated with the presence of a group of young males of persistent criminal habits who were clearly socially 'rootless' and 'drifting'. No such excess of single men appeared among the murder-suicide offenders.

A sample of ordinary suicides in London[1] showed conspicuously fewer married women than the national average, which was an opposite trend to the female sections of both the murder and the murder-suicide samples. On the other hand, Sainsbury's suicides showed a similar excess in the category of separated or divorced women, and some excess of separated or divorced men, but not so marked as in either the murder or murder-suicide samples. There was also an excess of widowers among the suicides, which did not appear in either the murder or murder-suicide samples. The deficit of married men among suicides was nothing like so extreme as in the case of the murderers.

Table 9 sets out the distribution of offenders by occupational class according to the Registrar-General's classification. In order to allocate as many individuals as possible to a class category, persons out of work or retired were classified according to their previous employment. Female offenders had to be omitted because so many were housewives and their husbands' occupations were not recorded. It is quite evident, however, that the murder sample had an excess of men of the lowest class V, the unskilled and casual labourers, compared with the general male population or with the Registrar-General's figures for men who commit suicide. The murder-suicide offenders, on the other hand, showed no evidence of shift towards the lower end of the class scale. (The apparent differences in Table 9 between the census distribution and the murder-suicide sample could not be considered significant in view of the small numbers involved and the absence of any consistent trend.)

Times of Murder

The time of day when murder occurs probably bears some relation to both the social and personal factors involved. (The possible association between depressive illness and murders in

---

[1] P. Sainsbury, *Suicide in London*, op. cit.

the early hours of the morning will be mentioned later.) In the present survey, no very striking contrasts appeared between the times chosen for murder-suicide and for ordinary murder. The time distribution, so far as it could be determined within the limitations of the data, is set out in Table 10. The most favoured times in both samples were late at night, rather more so in the case of ordinary murder than in murder followed by suicide. Such differences in this respect as were evident between the two samples were connected with the fact that the sample of ordinary murders were predominantly male offenders, and whereas most men killed at night most women killed during the day.

Rather more interesting was the comparison of days of the week on which the incidents took place. In communities in which many murders are associated with heavy drinking, one expects a peak incidence at weekends or on pay days. Fuentes in a survey in Santiago, Chile, compared 136 incidents of murder and 225 suicides not connected with murder. He found that 41% of the murders, but only 26% of the suicides, took place on Saturday or Sunday.[1]

Wolfgang, in his Philadelphia survey, found that homicides were much more frequent on Fridays, Saturdays and Sundays (especially on Saturdays) than on other days of the week. This trend was most noticeable in negro males. In white females, however, of whom there were relatively few, the trend was reversed, more crimes occurring from Monday to Thursday than from Friday to Saturday.[2] Other American studies have shown a similar distribution; Harlan, in a report on 500 homicides in Birmingham, Alabama, found that over half occurred on Saturdays or Sundays, and that the peak was still more noticeable among negroes, probably because the Saturday night drinking spree was even more of a tradition among lower class negroes than among whites.[3]

Suicide statistics generally show an opposite trend, incidence being lowest at the weekend and highest at the commencement of the working week. Durkheim pointed this out in relation to the large sample of 6,587 suicides analysed by Guerry. 30·19%

---

[1] 'Statistical Information,' *Internat. Criminal Police Review*, 1961
[2] op. cit.
[3] 'Five Hundred Homicides,' *Journ. Criminal Law, Criminol. and Police Sc.*, 1950

of the total suicides took place on Monday or Tuesday, only 24·76% on Saturday or Sunday.[1]

Table 11 shows the days of the week on which the incidents included in this survey took place. The figures were compiled on the assumption that in the absence of any evidence to the contrary, incidents reported to have happened in the bedroom during the night probably occurred after midnight. In the sample of ordinary murders, incidents took place with much the same frequency on each day of the week, Saturdays and Sundays being in no way outstanding. In the sample of murders followed by suicide, however, incidents were conspicuously more frequent at the beginning of the working week, especially on Mondays. This cyclic variation was clearly associated with the exacerbation of illness liable to occur when women sufferers from depression are left alone at home after the weekend, and men sufferers find themselves unfit to cope with a normal weekly routine. In the main sample of murder-suicides, 8 out of the 28 offenders classed as presumptively insane by virtue of depressive illness committed their murders on a Monday, and one other killed on the Tuesday following a bank holiday Monday. That there was no post weekend peak in the sample of ordinary murders was a little curious, considering that nearly a half of these offenders (74 out of 156) were declared insane or of diminished responsibility, and many of these must have been suffering from depressive illness. However, the results of this analysis plainly showed that in this respect the murder-suicide cases followed a trend characteristic of suicide and untypical of murder.

Finally, seasonal incidence needs to be considered, since various investigators have remarked upon the increase in frequency of both homicide and suicide in the spring. Capstick refers to 'the well-known spring increase in the number of suicides' in this country,[2] and Sainsbury in his study of suicide in London notes that 'suicide is commonest in early summer'.[3] Monthly incidence figures for suicides are given for the United Kingdom and other countries by the World Health Organization (1961). Some monthly incidence figures for crimes

[1] *Suicide*, 1951 (trans. 1952)
[2] 'Urban and Rural Suicide,' *Journ. Mental Science*, 1960
[3] *Suicide in London*

initially recorded as murder in England and Wales have been published in Hansard (1959) and the Home Office Research Unit has kindly extended these to cover a 7-year period. Table 12 shows the distribution of homicides and suicides through four seasonal quarters, taking March-April-May as the salient spring quarter. A slightly increased incidence in springtime appears in both types of incident, but the murder-suicides have a peculiarity all of their own, namely a considerably increased frequency in the mid-summer months, and a decreased frequency in the autumn. It is doubtful whether any particular significance should be attached to this unexpected statistic, which does not seem to correspond to any relevant variable.

Criminal Histories

Offenders with previous convictions were few in the murder-suicide sample (17 men and 2 women, i.e. 13% of the total of 148) but considerably more numerous in the murder sample (72 men and 2 women, i.e. 47% of the total of 156 offenders). The simple statistic of absence or presence of a criminal record is a rather crude way of classifying offenders. It is slightly more informative to subdivide the offenders with a previous con-viction into those with a conviction for violence and those without.[1] It then appears that, at least as far as male offenders are concerned, previous criminal convictions, both for violent and non-violent offences are very much more frequent in the murder sample.

The high incidence of criminal records among offenders in the murder sample was partly due to some cases completely without parallel in the murder-suicide series, in which habitual criminals killed their victims, occasionally with the aid of accomplices, in the course of some other crime, such as robbery. Out of the 148 incidents making up the murder sample, 5 involved more than one convicted offender. (In 3 cases there were 2 offenders, and in 2 others there were 3 and 4 offenders respectively.) As might have been expected, all these 13 accomplices in crime were men, and all their victims were males unrelated to them. Four of these 5 incidents were typical of murders associated with predatory crimes (one shooting in a pay office, one waylaying with intent to rob, one fatal injury

[1] See Table 13.

to a night porter during a burglary, and one killing of a person who resisted robbery of a shop). The average age of the 11 offenders was 21, and only one was over 24. All of them had been previously convicted, only two had less than three convictions, and between them they had a total of 49 convictions, mostly for offences against property. The fifth incident was quite exceptional and untypical, being motivated by sexual jealousy, perpetrated by two offenders of mature age with no previous convictions, the services of the accomplice having been enlisted by means of false representations.

In addition to the 11 young men, all with previous convictions, whose responsibility for killing in the furtherance of theft was shared with accomplices, a further 12 men in the murder sample killed their victims in the course of robbery, burglary or similar crimes. Nine of these had been previously convicted and a tenth had been charged with housebreaking but acquitted. These 12 also were all young males, with an average age of 21. Four of them were in their 'teens, the oldest was 30 and the youngest 15. Incidentally, in at least two instances among the murders committed by these offenders accomplices were involved who were not convicted of murder.

The observation that murder in the course of other crime is practically exclusively a male phenomenon, and is committed by a younger group of offenders than the commoner domestic type murders, is nothing new. In the survey of homicides in Philadelphia Wolfgang showed that the homicides which took place during the commission of other felonies were all committed by males, two-thirds of whom were under 25 years of age, which was significantly younger than the remainder of the offenders in his sample.[1] The relevant point in this context is that this more or less distinct group of young offenders, most of whom have a previous criminal record, does not make an appearance in the sample of murders followed by suicide.

Discussions about murders associated with other offences usually concentrate on those committed in the furtherance of theft, particularly since such crimes have been defined as Capital Murder in the Homicide Act, 1957. However, killings which take place in association with sexual assaults are also sometimes the product of ruthlessly self-seeking and aggressive

[1] op. cit.

criminals. In the present murder sample there were 11 men who killed in conjunction with sexual crime, in order to subdue an unwilling victim of sexual assault, to forestall detection, or (as in one instance) to satisfy sadistic lust. These also had no analogue in the murder-suicide sample. Eight of these offenders attacked women, the other 3 killed small children. Nine of these sex murderers had been previously convicted, 3 of them having convictions for both sexual offences and crimes against property.

Whatever may have been the nature of the sexual mal-adjustments responsible for their behaviour, it seems likely that it was their generally aggressive and criminal propensities which led to the actual killing.

To summarize, 34 offenders in the murder series, that is 21·8%, killed in the furtherance of crimes, sexual or otherwise, and of these 29 had a previous criminal record. These murders were quite different in circumstance and motivation from anything met with in the murder-suicide sample. Unlike murders committed in a domestic setting, none of these crimes was followed by attempts to commit suicide, except in one instance, a homosexual man who took a small boy of 7 to a bomb site and then killed him when he began to cry. A few days later he committed buggery with another boy of 13 and then tried to kill both himself and his victim with gas.

Of the 34 males who killed while occupied on other crimes, only one was found insane. He was a mentally retarded offender who had killed a small boy after sexual molestation. This provides still further evidence of the distinction between 'domestic' murders on the one hand, which are likely to be committed by the mentally abnormal, and murders in the furtherance of other crimes, which are likely to be committed by habitual criminals who are not insane. It is relevant to note, however, that this group of criminal murders included only 40% of the total of male offenders with a criminal record.

In the case of the women murderers only 2 out of the 18 in the sample had an official criminal record, although there were 4 who might have been regarded as 'criminal types'. These 4, who were the only women in the murder sample who were held to be legally sane and sentenced for their crime, all showed violent or criminal propensities to a degree not met with at all among the women of the murder-suicide sample. One stabbed her husband to death during a quarrel over her Lesbianism, and another homosexual murderess stabbed a woman neighbour when she found her in bed with her female lover. The third woman was in violent dispute with her husband and she murdered a small girl apparently intending to put the blame on him. The fourth woman murdered her daughter-in-law after a series of violent quarrels. Of these 4 'criminal' women, one was a former brothel-keeper and had been previously charged with the murder of a female relative in the course of a quarrel, another had a series of convictions including charges of larceny, malicious damage and child neglect, and a third (the one who killed her husband) was known to have both alcoholic and Lesbian tendencies. All 4 were of aggressive and quarrelsome disposition.

Mental Illness

Apart from the minority of murders committed by criminal types for typically criminal motives, the bulk of the murder sample consisted of incidents very similar to those in the murder-suicide study, in which mental illness and domestic discord led to a final desperate outburst. For example, of the 18 women offenders in the murder sample, 14 were obviously mentally ill and were found either insane or unfit to plead. Of these 14, one was in a state of neurotic depression when she killed a very aged mother whom she had been trying to look after for a year. The other 13 all killed their own children. Apart from one with an isolated conviction for shop-lifting, all of these mentally disturbed women murderers were free from previous convictions. Nine of these women had attempted suicide at the time of the crime. From the particulars given, the evidence was usually convincing as regards the presence of a severe mental illness, although sometimes the diagnosis was less clear. The descriptions given (e.g. 'very depressed and threatening suicide over the last six months', and 'acute mental depression and very suicidal for ten months', 'treatment for neurotic breakdown with suicidal tendencies', 'certified patient in mental hospital following a suicidal attempt', 'extreme depression with religious delusions of evil', 'treated in hospital for acute anxiety state and suicidal condition') strongly suggested that the majority of these women were suffering from severe forms of depressive illness, although some were stated to be schizophrenic.

The murders committed by men fell almost as neatly into two contrasting groups. In the 'criminal' group, made up of 34 men who killed in conjunction with robberies or sexual assaults, nearly all the victims were strangers or at best acquaintances, and only one of the offenders was said to be suicidal. A group of 'predominantly domestic' murders was committed by the remaining 104 male offenders. They nearly all murdered either relatives or persons with whom they were intimate, and a third of them were reported to have suicidal tendencies. (Fifteen men attempted suicide immediately after committing murder, one procured poison intending to kill himself but lacked the courage and gave himself up to the police instead, and a further 16 were known to have made previous suicidal attempts or threats). In contrast to the group of 34 'criminal' murderers, only one of whom was declared insane, these 104 predominantly 'domestic' murderers included a high proportion of mentally abnormal persons. In fact a majority of them (59 out of 104) were found insane, unfit to plead or of 'diminished responsibility'. The psychiatric conditions from which they were suffering, so far as these could be inferred from the particulars on record, consisted of depression, personality disorder and schizophrenia in descending order of frequency. The associated circumstances, as well as the mental state of the offender, was very often essentially identical to that found in many cases in the murder-suicide series. The following case, typical of many in the murder sample, an instance of family slaughter by an insane depressive, was indistinguishable from similar cases in the murder-suicide study:

Case 522
A middle-aged man, happily married for many years, began to show symptoms of depressive illness. After a long period under his doctor, he was admitted to a mental hospital, where he was in a very agitated state, suffering from delusions that people were against him, and anxiously preoccupied with ideas that he was not doing the right thing for his child's welfare. He was finally discharged recovered after a year of severe illness and several serious suicidal attempts. Two years later, he again grew 'moody'

and 'strange', and developed delusions that people were talking against him and that his child was being affected in some way. While in this state, he attacked his wife and child with a knife, and attempted to kill himself with the same weapon. On subsequent examination, he moaned and wept, answered only in a very slow whisper, and was confused and often irrelevant in his replies to questions. It appeared that he had murdered his family, of whom he was very fond, with the intention that they should all die together. He had a criminal record – a single petty offence of larceny many years previously – but was found unfit to plead.

The above example was typical of murders inspired by melancholia, such as often, but not always, precede suicide. In contrast, here is another case, also from the murder sample, of a killing inspired by more characteristically criminal motives and committed by a sane offender, a type of incident rarely followed by suicide:

Case 523
A young man with a history of several convictions for crimes of dishonesty was separated from his wife and lodging with an elderly woman. Like so many criminals, he was a man of somewhat unstable personality, prone to bouts of drunkenness, unable to remain in any job for long because of an urge to move on, and strikingly deficient in lasting friendships or lasting affection for his wife or for any of the other women with whom he had associated. He was moody and aggressive and had been told he had a 'chip on his shoulder'.

He had various altercations with his landlady. One day he attacked and killed her, hid the weapon, and then denied all knowledge of how she had met her death. His exact motives were not proved, although it was known he had stolen from the landlady, and he may have wanted to avoid exposure, or he may have simply lost control of his temper when reprimanded.

Points of Similarity and Contrast
The most important ways in which murders preceding suicide differed from other murders may be summarized as follows. Among ordinary murderers a significant minority consisted of offenders who killed in connection with other crimes, notably robbery, burglary and sexual assault, and their victims were nearly all strangers or casual acquaintances. These offenders

were all men, often very young men, most of them had a criminal record, virtually all of them were legally sane, and many of them had carried out their murders with accomplices. Such cases hardly ever occurred among the murder-suicides. The murder-suicides were almost entirely domestic crimes, mothers killing their young children or men killing their wives or mistresses. Relatively few of the murder-suicide offenders had a criminal record (13% compared with 47%), more of them were 40 years of age or over (52% compared with 24%), more of them were women (40% compared with 11%), and many more of them killed their own children (47% compared with 16%).

In spite of these contrasts there was also considerable overlap, in that the group of ordinary murders included many cases similar to the typical murder-suicides. In both groups, almost half the offenders were psychiatrically abnormal to a degree sufficient for jury verdicts of 'insanity' or 'diminished responsibility', and in both groups depressive illness was a common diagnosis, and especially so in the female offenders. Whereas the number of sane offenders in the murder group was swollen by the presence of a proportion of young criminals, the number of sane offenders among the murder-suicides was largely accounted for by those apparently normal persons who, when they or their families were faced with great stress (such as incurable illness or threatened disgrace) chose to end their own lives and those of their loved ones at the same time. In connection with the family murders it was evident that some of the offenders, both in the murder group and among the murder-suicides, had a previous history of violence, directed either against themselves or against others. Twelve offenders in the murder sample (7·7%) were reported to have made definite suicidal attempts in the past, and as many again had made suicidal threats. In the murder-suicide sample, 15% were reported to have made a previous suicidal attempt. Crimes that represented the culmination of years of domestic violence were not uncommon, both in the murder group and the murder-suicide sample. Although such histories provided an indication of the violent propensities of some of these domestic offenders, relatively few had actually been convicted by the courts for crimes of violence.

By and large the few published reports from other countries show rather similar trends in the differences between murder and murder-suicide. Wolfgang compared his sample of murder-suicides with the total sample of criminal homicides. In spite of having only a small number of the former, he demonstrated several interesting statistical differences, all tending to suggest that the murder-suicide cases deviated less markedly than ordinary murderers from the standards and attitudes of the normal law-abiding community. For example, in the murder-suicide sample alcohol was present in either victim or offender in a significantly smaller proportion of cases (3 in 10 compared with 6 or 7 in 10), a significantly smaller proportion were negroes (1 in 2 compared with 3 in 4), a record of previous arrest was also significantly less frequent (1 in 3 compared with nearly 2 in 3) but a significantly higher proportion of these crimes were committed at the home of either the offender or his victim (5 in 6 compared with 1 in 2) and nearly all involved intimate personal relationships between offender and victim. The median age of the murder-suicide offenders was 7 years older than that of ordinary homicides. These observations suggested that murder-suicides tend to be committed by individuals of relatively normal character development (super-ego), acting under the stress of acutely frustrating circumstances, usually severe conflict with an individual to whom the offender is very attached. Having a strong super-ego these offenders subsequently suffer pronounced guilt reactions. 'Suicide thus becomes a means of showing his agreement with the social norms which he has long ago internalized.' In conformity with the hypothesis that only the most severe frustration, followed by the most violent upsurge of aggression, would provoke such persons to kill, Wolfgang found that killings followed by suicide were significantly more often unduly violent (multiple stabbing and shooting) than ordinary homicides.[1]

On the basis simply of published statistics, and without benefit of individual case studies, the American murder-suicide incidents described by Cavan and Wolfgang obviously differ greatly from what commonly occurs in this country. In part, this merely reflects the considerable contrasts between the two

[1] op. cit.

countries in regard to murder in general. The incidence of insanity among American murderers is comparatively low, only 3·2% in Wolfgang's sample. Also noteworthy in America is the small proportion of child victims of murder. In the Philadelphia study less than 6% were under 16,[1] so it is not particularly surprising that only one child appeared among the 26 victims of murder-suicide in that city. In England about one-third of all murder victims are under 16, a fact clearly linked with the observation that in England 80% of women murderers kill their own children. In England, two-thirds of all murderers have no record of any previous criminal convictions, whereas in Philadelphia only about one-third were free from a previous arrest record. So it is not surprising to find much fewer murder-suicide offenders with criminal records in England than in Philadelphia.

Granting that the differing character of homicides in the two countries means one starts making comparisons from different base lines, the fact remains that the type and direction of the contrasts between murder and murder-suicide are rather similar in England and Philadelphia. As regards age, choice of victim and history of previous convictions murder-suicide offenders in both countries are less criminal, more intimately related to their victims and (at least among the males) of maturer age than ordinary murderers. One discrepant observation concerned the sex of offenders. In England murder-suicide offenders have a relatively high proportion of women, but in the Philadelphia study, where the proportion of women among all homicide offenders was 1 in 6, among murder-suicides it was only 1 in 12. A complicating factor may have been that in Philadelphia 85% of women murderers were negroes, and one suspects that they would be less prone to suicide than whites of either sex.

A point to which Wolfgang drew attention was that suicide in Philadelphia less often followed the murder of a husband by his wife (one case only out of a total of 47) than the murder of a wife by her husband (10 cases in a total of 53). From Tables 32 and 33 of the Gibson and Klein report[2] one sees that in England, out of 131 husbands who killed their wives, 55 (42%) killed

[1] op. cit., ii, 1958, Table 1, p. 361
[2] op. cit.

themselves, whereas out of 12 women who killed their husbands 6 (50%) committed suicide. Wolfgang argued that wives in Philadelphia probably felt less guilty than husbands after the slaying of a spouse, since wives usually do this only after much provocation. Perhaps English wives feel differently about their husbands!

The statistical study of Danish homicides by Siciliano yielded figures in many respects closer to those of England than Wolfgang's sample.[1] In Denmark, killings by violent or predatory criminals, who are usually young males, form an even smaller proportion of all murders than is the case in England. Murder is very predominantly a domestic affair in Denmark, only 18·7% of victims being killed by other than their lovers or members of their families, whereas in England the proportion is a little over a third and in Philadelphia about two-thirds.[2] In all three countries, women murderers in particular tend to kill their lovers or members of the family, 86·5% in the case of white women in Philadelphia, 94% in the case of English women, and 97·5% in the case of Danish women. Consequently, the varying proportions of women among murderers (a third in Denmark, a fifth in England and a sixth in Philadelphia) account for some of the differences between the patterns of murder in these communities. Siciliano found that in Denmark 59% of homicides were family tragedies, that is killing of spouse or children, and that 44% of all victims were under 12 years of age (practically all of these children being murdered by their own parents), and that 85% of those who killed their children subsequently committed suicide. He concluded that the commonest type of homicide in Denmark was 'a woman in the 25 to 40 age group, with one or two children under 12, who gasses them and herself out of despair or depression'. Thus it would seem that the statistical trends associated with murder-suicide in England characterize the whole homicide pattern in Denmark. Unfortunately Siciliano does not give separate figures for the Danish murder-suicide cases, but one can deduce from the information given that a half of this group of offenders are women and that 85% of the cases involve the killing of children. One may fairly conclude that

[1] op. cit.
[2] op. cit., ii, 1958; Table 24, p. 207

among this group there are even fewer criminal types than among Danish murderers who come to trial.

As far as they go, the statistics available in these three communities all fit the hypothesis that murderers who kill themselves, compared with murderers in general, form a less socially deviant group, and that their relationships to their victims are more often close and intimate.

V

Murder-Suicide by 'Normal' Persons

IN this and subsequent chapters the murder-suicide cases are considered in greater detail, with particular reference to the main sample of 78 instances studied individually. A substantial proportion of the offenders in the main sample were relatively ordinary individuals, free from taint of previous criminality and, so far as superficial appearances went, not suffering from any definite mental illness, and certainly not psychotic. Some of these offenders had given way to their desperate crime only after a period of considerable stress, occasioned by extreme conflict situations or by extraordinarily trying domestic situations.

Norwood East, in discussing murders committed by normal persons, wrote: 'Murder is rather frequently due to an intensely emotional situation operating suddenly upon a man who has always behaved in a perfectly normal manner except for the few seconds in his life when the murder is committed.'[1] As an example he cited the case of a man who quarrelled with a girl with whom he had just had sexual intercourse. He found she had recently been with another man, and he concluded that she had only agreed to intercourse with him as a ruse for fixing paternity upon him in the event of pregnancy. In the heat of the ensuing quarrel, he struck her fatally with a chopper, after which he struck himself on the head with the same weapon, flaking off a portion of skull, but failing to kill himself. Subsequently he displayed sincere grief at the girl's death, and after his reprieve he continued well-behaved, industrious and rational as he had always been. This group of murderers of respectable antecedents and ordinary standards of conduct accounts for the commonplace experience that many

[1] W. Norwood East, *Society and the Criminal*, H.M.S.O., London, 1949, p. 275

imprisoned murderers give little trouble to the authorities and often seem much 'nicer types' than other convicts.

Among the 78 murder-suicide cases studied individually were many instances in which the crime stood out as an unexpected and exceptional outburst in an otherwise ordinary, well-controlled life. In such cases the precipitating events were always very obvious, the victims were always the murderer's own family or intimates, and the conscious motives at least were often altruistic. In a number of these cases the victims may have acquiesced in their own deaths. The sort of circumstances commonly associated with these murders are illustrated in the following example:

Case 15

A married couple, both of them nearly 80 years of age and living on their own, were unwell and finding it very difficult to fend for themselves. The wife had influenza and bronchitis, the husband had bronchitis and advanced cardiovascular disease and would not have had long to live.

One morning the husband hit his wife a powerful blow over the head with a hammer from behind and then strangled her, after which he took poison. The preparation of a recent will not mentioning the wife, and the purchase of the poison in advance, suggested some previous planning. An unexpected caller discovered the murderer before the poison had fully taken effect. The murderer answered questions lucidly, explaining that the victim had been a very good wife to him, that he had been ill a long time and that he had done it 'out of loyalty' and that they 'had an understanding'.

The family doctor knew the couple well and confirmed that the old man had been a devoted husband. He had led a full, active life and was an intelligent and resolute character. Almost certainly he had weighed up their poor prospects, perhaps even discussed them with his wife, and then taken action.

Especially among elderly male offenders, there was sometimes clear association between murder-suicide incidents and failing health or painful physical disease, as in the above example. According to medical evidence, including post-mortem findings, over a quarter of the 78 offenders (13 men and 8 women) were ill or suffering from some physical disability at the time of the crime. In this respect, the murder-suicide cases were no different from ordinary suicides, to which physical illness, and especially terminal conditions of the elderly, make a significant contribution. The actual illnesses of the offenders ranged from a number of cases of advanced cancer or heart disease, to such conditions as severe asthma or skin disease in which psychogenic factors may have been important.

Sometimes the health of the victims was a definite consideration. Of the 50 adult victims, 6 were aged sick with very little expectation of life remaining (Cases 5, 9, 15, 31, 38 and 78), and some of the others had severe mental or physical handicaps. Specifically, one was an imbecile, three were cardiac semi-invalids (Cases 29, 32 and 40), two others had recently been in mental hospital, another was a drug addict (Case 4), and another (Case 28) was suffering from a post-traumatic neurosis manifested by complaints of unbearable headache, threats of suicide, and violent rages. Among the child victims, two were mental defectives (Cases 39 and 45), one of them with mongol deformity, and at least three had severe neurosis or behaviour disturbance.

The element of 'mercy killing' of a helpless, or supposedly helpless victim, which was fairly evident in Case 15, quoted above, was more obvious still in several cases, such as the following:

Case 5
A bachelor in his fifties had always lived with and cared for a nagging, possessive mother. She was now well into her eighties, for many years a bed-ridden arthritic cripple, and completely dependent upon him. He was found to have an inoperable cancer, and was supposed to go into hospital, but his old mother was reluctant for him to leave. Early on the morning his departure was due, he stuffed rags under the door, turned on the gas, and they both died. There was no sign of struggle, but the old woman would not have been able to move from her bed even if she had tried to do so.

In another particularly sad case of 'mercy killing' the offender misjudged the seriousness of his victim's illness:

Case 29
An elderly man, generally regarded as a quiet, patient character and a devoted husband, was greatly concerned about 'heart

attacks' experienced by his wife. Actually her condition was not dangerous, her symptoms, though distressing, being exaggerated by a neurotic tendency. He shot her dead in the middle of the night, and then killed himself the same way. A brief suicide note explained that he had done this to free her from pain. Apart from his obvious preoccupation with his wife's health, there was no indication in the offender's demeanour, or in his medical history, of the impending tragedy, although the statements left behind indicated some premeditation.

Misguided altruism would seem to be a common feature of many of the murder-suicides committed by outwardly normal persons acting under circumstances of special stress. Several examples of the kind were mentioned in the previous section when possible suicide pacts were being discussed. But aggressive motives, sometimes well concealed and sometimes quite undisguised, were also evident in some cases. The following example displays an all too familiar theme. The rejected lover first threatens suicide, then a little later turns his violence against his mistress as well as himself. He does not openly admit his love has turned to hate, but says they could not bear to be parted:

Case 65
A working man had a sexual affair with a young woman considerably above him in social class. In response to her family's protests, she decided to end the association. This led to some violent quarrels during which he threatened to shoot himself. Finally he appeared to agree to their parting, only to return the day following and shoot her dead and then himself. His suicide note explained that they could not be happy without each other and he had decided to take her with him.

In the next case, in which children were murdered by their mother, the crime was probably at least in part an act of aggression against a neglectful husband.

Case 13
A middle-aged couple, living outwardly well regulated and highly respectable lives, had been in a state of marital discord for many years. The husband chose employment activities that took him away frequently, and his family interests, as manifest in conversations with friends and in letters home, were clearly directed

more towards his children than his wife. She complained of his coldness and neglect, and had once threatened to leave, although at the same time she took up various activities and interests in an effort to please him. People who knew her well, who saw her immediately before the murder, noticed nothing unusual. She was a strongly built, intelligent and determined woman. While her husband was away, having prepared the ground with a hose-pipe lead and a cushion up the chimney, she gassed herself and her children – who were at an age at which a certain amount of force had to be exerted in order to subdue them.

In the next example, also committed by an offender who would generally have been described as 'normal' by his associates, the rage of the rejected lover was quite obvious, as was the progressive inclusiveness of his violent impulses, directed first against himself alone, and then against his girl-friend.

Case 54
An ambitious young man, busily engaged with a professional career, had been unsuccessfully trying to persuade a girl-friend to marry him. Becoming despondent about some examinations, and having had a particularly serious row with his girl-friend, he attempted suicide with gas. This having failed, he went out and bought a gun, called on the girl and shot her dead, and then shot himself. He left behind a suicide note which contained recriminations against her for the way she had treated him.

The next example, in which the crime was apparently com-mitted on account of a wife's desertion, was of special interest because a long time before the offender had made a suicidal attempt under rather similar circumstances:

Case 47
For some time the offender had been looking after his children on his own, his wife having left him for another man. She had returned to him briefly, but left again, and on the night of her departure the offender said he was going to go after her and the other man and murder them both. In fact he went looking for her, but did not find her, and on returning home he killed his small children and himself with gas. Some ten years previously he had made a serious suicidal attempt when his girl-friend broke

off their engagement. He was found unconscious in the street outside her home, having swallowed some poison. After being revived on that occasion he said he had nothing to live for and wished that he had been allowed to die.

In a few cases, the offenders belonged to a social class or sub-culture in which a certain degree of violence passed as normal. In the following example, the offender's associates found no reason to regard him as unusual or abnormal in spite of a history of violent marital disputes arising from sexual infidelity.

Case 46
The offender had been living with a young woman who had deserted her husband. They quarrelled when she became friendly with another married man, and he with another woman. He left her, and in return she threatened to kill him. He called back to see her, ostensibly to collect some belongings. Subsequently they were found sitting together, both dead, with gunshot wounds in the head. On the basis of the pathologist's evidence, it was concluded that the woman's wound was not self-inflicted, and that she had been murdered. A police report commented that in view of the relaxed position of the bodies they might have both died voluntarily.

In some cases the circumstances leading to the crime appeared comparatively innocuous, and it remained a mystery why an apparently normal individual should react so badly:

Case 67
A middle-aged man, who had worked satisfactorily for the same firm all his life, was detected in a trivial theft from his place of employment. He was asked to leave. He was not in financial difficulty, but was noticed to be unduly anxious, even though his employers promised not to prosecute.

A few days after, he murdered his wife and then killed himself. Relatives testified that they had always seemed devoted, and lived a quiet, uneventful existence. The wife was subject to chronic worrying and depression about her health and her children, but this was not felt to be unusual.

In this case one might suspect that the onset of stealing in a previously respectable and conscientious middle-aged man heralded some emotional change, perhaps even a depressive illness, but information bearing upon this possibility was not obtainable.

Some of the offenders classed as apparently 'normal' nevertheless showed a certain degree of neurotic disturbance, but not sufficient to mark them as seriously abnormal in the eyes of their acquaintances, or to distinguish them in psychiatric terms from the substantial percentage of similarly affected persons in the general population. In the next example, although the crime was precipitated by an obvious environmental stress, the offender's own weaknesses of character and neurotic symptoms had contributed to produce both the predicament and the catastrophic reaction to it:

Case 72
The offender was a middle-aged man, described as 'quiet, hesitant and decent living', little is known of his mental state except that he had a marked stammer and was suffering from some nervous trouble for which he was under treatment by his doctor. On account of this he was frequently absent from his employment, which in turn led to shortage of money and difficulty in meeting hire-purchase commitments on his furniture. He tried ineffectively to escape from his difficulties through money-lenders.

When the situation got so bad that he was threatened with loss of his home, he gassed his wife and children as they lay in bed at night, and then killed himself. A number of suicide notes written just before he died explained what he had done, complained bitterly about the hopelessness of his situation, said that he was taking his wife and children with him to save them from scandal, and made numerous scathing and vindictive references to his creditors. He also damaged some of his possessions so that the creditors should derive no benefit.

In some cases, especially in those which arose from a background of chronic marital discord, it was obvious that the victim's peculiarities of temperament were at least as important in the situation as the offender's. In the following example the offender was considered to be fairly described as 'normal', but his wife's behaviour was not above suspicion:

Case 78
An elderly couple had recently moved their home so that the husband, who was retired, might take up some part-time work.

Unfortunately the job he had expected did not materialize, as a result of which he spent a lot of time in the house.

His wife had always been hasty tempered and a persistent nagger, and relatives noticed that he allowed her to refer to him disparagingly without protest, and that she habitually went out in pursuit of her own work and interests leaving him to fend for himself. She was an emotionally cold person. They occupied separate rooms, and it was always left to the husband to communicate with their only child, a married son living some distance away. The wife had had medical treatment for 'nervous debility' and eczema. In contrast, the husband was a generally lively, sociable character, but in later years, although he made no complaint, he seemed rather cowed. Shortly before his death, the wife remarked to an acquaintance that her husband had changed recently, become depressed, and asked her not to go out and leave him. A letter recently written to his son showed that he was concerned about his health and made some reference to an uncertain future.

This was the situation when, without any warning so far as friends and relatives could say, he violently attacked and killed his wife and then himself while they were alone in the house.

Altogether, 33 of the 78 cases in the main sample were murders and suicides committed by seemingly sane persons, many of whom never had been treated by a psychiatrist and, so far as could be ascertained, had never had any kind of mental breakdown. Although considerable antecedent stress and emotional turmoil must have been present in most of these offenders, many of them showed minimal disturbance in outward behaviour before committing their crime, and consequently their desperate action could not have been foreseen by an ordinary observer. In this respect, these cases resemble the majority of successful suicides in England, many of which are committed by outwardly normal persons whose demeanour arouses no suspicion of danger. Parnell and Skottowe found that only one-fifth of their series of 100 suicides had ever been in mental hospital.[1] Capstick found that only 17·7% of 881 suicides had been referred to a psychiatrist or admitted to hospital.[2] In over one-third of Capstick's series the potential suicide behaved normally just before death, although

[1] 'Towards Preventing Suicide,' *The Lancet*, 1957
[2] op. cit.

many had made deliberate preparations and written suicide notes while preserving an outward appearance of equanimity. Nevertheless, very few such cases were inexplicable, in the sense that no reason for the person's desperate frame of mind could be discovered. Depressive ideas were particularly frequent in the elderly; outwardly aggressive motives occurred more often in those under 30 years of age, a few of whom left behind suicide notes revealing anger and malice against others, such as the one which read, 'I'm sick of slaving for Dad, a mean and ungrateful man.'

In brief, murder-suicides by sane persons acting under stress bear a quite striking similarity to ordinary cases of suicide. The precipitating stresses have much in common, notably despair and hopelessness in the aged sick, impulsive aggression of young persons in the throes of frustrating and ambivalent love affairs, or inability to bear the discovery of financial or sexual deceits. The overt motives and attendant circumstances of suicide and of murder-suicide are in fact so similar that it seems a fair presumption that many of the latter are of the nature of suicides extended to involve an innocent victim rather than murders followed by suicide as an after-thought of fear or remorse. This distinction will be discussed in greater detail later, after the crimes committed by mentally abnormal offenders have been described.

VI

Criminal Types among Murder-Suicides

A WELL recognized group among murderers consists of offenders aptly termed 'criminal types', in that they resemble closely the general run of predatory criminals. That is to say, they are reckless, anti-social individuals who readily resort to physical violence, to subdue an opponent in a quarrel, to facilitate robbery, or to escape capture. Mostly they are uneducated persons of primitive attitudes and poor social background. Banay has described them as the 'sub-cultural' group of murderers.[1] They belong to the under-privileged sectors of the community, and their social and ethical development has been stunted by adverse environmental circumstances. As an example, Banay quoted the case of a murderer who had responded to a blow – struck in the course of a quarrel over a woman – by drawing a knife and stabbing his assailant to death. The killer came from a deprived home. He had lost his parents as a small boy. Later he had lived with a woman from a drunken and generally immoral family. She proved unfaithful, abusive and neglectful of their children. The readiness with which persons habituated to this inferior style of living resort to physical violence, combined with the aggressiveness aroused by his frustrating domestic situation, went some way to explain this man's disproportionate reaction to provocation. Banay placed in this 'sub-cultural' category most acquisitive killings, murders in the course of robbery, and murders committed to escape arrest.

Countries with a high murder ratio usually have a high proportion of murderers of the 'criminal type', armed robbers and burglars being the commonest examples of the type.[2] One

---

[1] 'Study in Murder,' *Annals Amer. Ac. Polit. Soc. Sc.*, 1952
[2] H. C. Brearley, *Homicide in the U.S.A.*, p. 81

expects such murderers to come from a criminal milieu, to have a history of previous convictions – for dishonesty if not for violence – and to have a fair number of the undesirable attitudes and character traits commonly described as psychopathic. Grunhut, basing his views on the Minutes of Evidence taken before the Royal Commission on Capital Punishment (1949), has suggested that this type of murderer has become relatively commoner in England in recent years.[1] Excluding those found insane, 58% of murderers convicted in England in the years 1940–49 belonged to this acquisitive, criminal group. Confirmation of the increasing frequency of this type appears in the Home Office study of murder which showed, in respect of murders known to the police, that the proportion of offenders with previous convictions has risen from 1955 to 1960 from a quarter to a third.[2]

On common-sense grounds one might expect the 'criminal type' of murder, especially cold-blooded crimes committed for gain, to occur infrequently in association with suicide. Havard has described one such case in which the murderer killed himself only when detection threatened. This was a man who poisoned his wife, while she was a patient in a sanatorium, by bringing her gifts of food laden with arsenic. When the true cause of her death unexpectedly came to light, and he was questioned by the police, he thereupon committed suicide.[3]

Examination of the present sample of murder-suicide cases amply confirmed the expectation that, compared with ordinary murders, very few were committed by persons with a criminal record, or by persons activated by motives of material gain. Out of the total 148 murder-suicide offenders only 19 (13%) had a record of previous criminal convictions. Even this modest figure is rather high compared with Gibson and Klein's national sample in which they found only 10 male offenders with previous convictions out of 222 suspects who committed suicide in the years 1955 to 1960.

For the purpose of assessing the importance of criminal background in murder-suicide offenders, this method of

[1] 'Murder and the Death Penalty in England,' p. 161, *Annals Amer. Ac. Polit. Soc. Sc.*, 1952
[2] op. cit., Table 37
[3] *The Detection of Secret Homicide* (London, 1960), p. 169

comparison is rather crude. It takes no account of the nature of the previous offences or their degree of relevance to the crime of murder, and it disregards the complicating factor of the high proportion of women among murder-suicide cases. In the sample of 78 murder-suicide cases which were studied in detail, the 'criminal types' were fairly easily identified. They were so few they can be enumerated one by one.

Of the 34 women offenders, not one could fairly be called a 'criminal type'. One woman (Case 70)[1] had actually had a conviction, but that was for shop-lifting ten years previously, an episode that seemed to have almost no bearing upon the murder-suicide incident. Furthermore, she was well known to be highly abnormal mentally and her doctor had tried many times in vain to persuade her to accept psychiatric attention.

Of the 44 male offenders, 10 had one or more previous convictions. One of these (Case 18) an immigrant, had had convictions for petty larceny some years before when still living in his own country, but at the time of his death he was a good-living citizen and his crime could not reasonably be held to have arisen from a criminal way of life.

In addition to those with a criminal record, 3 other men (Cases 8, 64 and 67) had been detected cheating their employers, but their dishonesty had not come to the notice of the police. Each of these killed himself and his wife while under threat of possible exposure. They were not included in the 'criminal' category since by no stretch of the imagination could the murders they committed be regarded as the natural outcome of ruthless or violent criminal careers. None of them had been convicted, or even faced with prosecution, and even had they lived they would probably never have appeared in any criminal statistic. The fact that they preferred death to facing shame set them still further apart from the general run of shameless law breakers.[2]

On the other hand, one man (Case 2), although he had no conviction officially recorded against him, was a known criminal and was 'wanted' by the police at the time he committed murder and suicide. This leaves 10 men in the sample, that is 23%

---

[1] A list of the cases quoted in this report, giving reference to the pages on which they occur, is set out in Appendix I.

[2] See p. 52 for an example of this type.

of the male offenders, who might reasonably be considered 'criminal types'. As might be expected of any small group of criminals classified psychiatrically, none were psychotic, the majority had personalities more or less within the range of normal variation, but a few were definitely psychopathic. These 10 cases will now be described. One case, unique in the sample, was a cold-blooded murder for gain comparable to the case quoted by Havard:

Case 12

In social status this man was unusually superior for a criminal. Although well-travelled, and a former officer of H.M. Forces, he had nevertheless been court martialled for theft and convicted on a dozen or more occasions in different countries for various frauds. He was of powerful physique and had some reputation for violence. He certainly lacked moral restraint in many spheres; for instance he was not only promiscuously adulterous but at one time insisted on importing a mistress into the marital home.

The life of his wife, from whom he had been separated for some time, stood between himself and a substantial fund of money. He made contact with her again for a short time and then killed her, planning the means carefully so as to simulate an accident in the bathroom, and taking such precautions as wiping off fingerprints and using a false passport. Despite these precautions he was taken by surprise when a relative of his wife's arrived and discovered what had happened. A great struggle ensued and he murdered this person also and then escaped for a few days. When it became clear that his guilt was known and he was threatened with arrest he first wrote some long, carefully worded instructions to his solicitors and then killed himself.

The next example was a typical aggressive psychopath, impulsively violent, of vain, unstable personality, and much given to rambling, confused statements and threats:

Case 22

A young man who had been convicted on four occasions, the last time for a violent assault, had been subject to tempers and smashing up the home ever since adolescence. He had been invalided from the forces as an aggressive psychopath. He subsequently refused medical help. He was divorced for adultery, and remarried at once. His second wife suffered much from his rages and was indeed severely thrashed on her honeymoon. Following one of his quarrels about money, he attacked his wife and two of her female relatives, smashing a chair over their heads. When the police came to see him he shot them and ran away. Hours later, when they were closing in, he shot himself.

Only one other 'criminal' case fell indisputably into the category of aggressive psychopath:

Case 40
A middle-aged married man had had unaccountable 'brainstorms' since childhood. His married life was one long quarrel. He had been convicted on eight occasions for stealing and fraud and had been sent to Borstal and on three occasions to prison. In addition he was an alcoholic and had once nearly lost his sight through taking methylated spirit. Although intelligent and decently educated and possessed of respectable relatives his personality was so unstable he was chronically out of work. For three years he and his family had been camping out in utter squalor on a small landing outside a flat from which they had been evicted. Early one morning, presumably during one of his habitual rages, he shot and killed the entire family.

One other man, though less extreme in his behaviour than the previous two, probably deserved the label aggressive psychopath:

Case 4
A middle-aged negro, described by an acquaintance as 'a violent man with a vicious temper', had several convictions for violence, including causing grievous bodily harm, and on another occasion being armed with an offensive weapon. In addition he was a peddler of narcotics. He lived with a woman who had recently been treated in hospital for drug addiction. She was also a convicted thief and prostitute. There were such frequent scenes of jealousy and violence between them that when he murdered her in the small hours one morning by repeated stabbing, the neighbours paid no attention to the screams and thuds.

Apart from the two just mentioned, 3 more of the 'criminal' types had had a conviction for violence. One of them (Case 24) had killed a woman friend 23 years previously and served a sentence for manslaughter. His final act was to suffocate his mistress and then swallow poison. Unfortunately, little could be discovered about him. He left no suicide note and his previous crime was too long ago for prison records to have been preserved.

Another example quoted later (Case 59, p. 18) was a budding young thug recently convicted for assault in connection with teen-age gang warfare. He shot his girl-friend for no very clear reason and later hanged himself. Her death could have been unintentional. Lastly, there was one man (Case 45) with four convictions – on three occasions for theft, once for assault – who was clearly a psychiatric case. He had been a patient in several mental hospitals, and at the inquest following his crime the verdict was returned that he had taken his son's life and his own 'owing to acute depressive psychosis'.

Three more 'criminal' cases remain unmentioned. One was the criminal who was 'wanted' by the police because he had been concerned in a haul of jewellery (Case 2, p. 23). As in Case 4 above, his victim was the woman he was cohabiting with, who was also his partner in crime, and their deaths were more like the result of a suicide pact than a murder. He left a note behind explaining that the game was up and asking to be buried with his victim, while she left behind some written confessions together with instructions that they should be sold to the press for the benefit of her surviving child.

In the next example the criminal was a typically inadequate, small-time crook, ordinarily passive and dependent, but provoked to desperation when his woman friend and support was removed:

Case 58

A single man in the late fifties, with 18 convictions for small-scale offences of larceny, shop-breaking, etc., had spent much of his life in prison. When at liberty he took such dubious employments as 'dealer' and 'bookmaker's runner'. He was described as gentle when sober but apt to knock women about when drunk. He had recently formed an attachment to a widow who allowed him to stay at her house. When she announced her intention to sell the house and remarry he became abusive. Finally he shot dead her fiancé and himself immediately after.

Only one more case remains:

Case 43

This was a young married man of lower working class origin. He was one of eleven children by a criminal father, who had been brought up under conditions both miserable and filthy. He had four convictions for petty larceny and had been to Borstal. In recent years, however, he had improved remarkably, giving up thieving and settling down to marriage and a steady job, but a probation officer observed that he had never learned to control his temper. He had many long and violent quarrels with his wife, who refused him sexual intercourse and insisted on going out to an evening job against his wishes. He stabbed her in the middle of the night and then gassed himself and their child.

It is of interest to note that, of the 10 male offenders here grouped as 'criminal types', all but one had some history of violent behaviour, although only 5 had actual convictions for violence. As will be seen later, especially when the mentally abnormal cases are discussed, proneness to violence appears to be a significant antecedent in a substantial number of murder-suicide offenders, although this is not necessarily associated either with criminal convictions for violence or with criminal associations and style of life.

As Morris and Blom-Cooper have recently pointed out,[1] convictions for offences against property, and minor violence in words and deeds, is commonplace in the lower-class milieu from which so many murderers are drawn, and may not be very relevant in an individual case. However, a history of serious domestic violence is a more important antecedent of murder than a history of having been convicted for some possibly irrelevant criminal offence.

---

[1] op. cit., p. 281

VII

Mental Abnormality in Murder-Suicide Offenders

(1) *Incidence Figures*

THE main sample of 78 murder-suicide offenders was examined as closely as possible for indications of mental abnormality among the offenders, either at the time of their deaths or previously. Contact with family doctors and with mental hospitals, besides giving additional information on the types of mental disturbance involved, also yielded evidence of abnormality in a number of cases in which this would not have been apparent from scrutiny of the police dossiers only.

A high proportion of the 78 offenders in the main sample were suffering from manifest psychiatric disorder at the time of their crime. Depression, either of the psychotic or the neurotic reactive type, was the commonest diagnosis, but cases of schizophrenia, psychopathy and severe neurosis were also found. There were no instances of obvious mental subnormality. Table 14 gives the numbers of abnormal offenders and how they were allocated to one or other of these conventional diagnostic classes. Unfortunately, mental abnormality is very much a matter of degree, and diagnostic standards, especially in connection with psychopathy and neurosis, are neither well defined nor generally agreed. How these patients are diagnosed, or whether they are deemed to fall within the range of normal variation and hence unworthy to receive any psychiatric label at all, depends at least as much on the individual doctor's attitude as it does on the patient's mental condition. In order to convey some impression of the standards used for the classification shown in Table 14, and the meaning of the diagnostic labels employed, some examples are quoted from each category.

Before going into details of individual cases, however, it may be of help to explain that of the 45 offenders considered psychiatrically abnormal, 39 were thought to have been so seriously disordered that they would likely have been found insane or of 'diminished responsibility' if they had survived to come before a jury. Most of these 39 'insane' offenders were suffering from an obvious psychotic illness, persons who had lost touch with reality and were voicing delusional ideas. The standards applied in guessing which offenders were 'insane' were necessarily subjective, but they probably erred on the side of excessive stringency in comparison with the way juries behave in practice, especially in the case of women murderers, of whom 95% of those brought to trial and not acquitted are found insane or of diminished responsibility. Possibly some of the cases nowadays found to be of diminished responsibility might formerly have pleaded successfully some form of pro-vocation which would have reduced their offence to one of manslaughter. Of the 39 offenders considered to be 'insane', so far as could be discovered only 16 had actually been seen by psychiatrists, the other 23 being either unwilling to accept help, or not recognized as seriously ill by those in contact with them. In the case of the 6 offenders with psychiatric disorder of lesser degree, considered insufficient to amount to 'insanity', opinions of family doctors or other responsible witnesses were available to the effect that they were known to be mentally abnormal.

Among the 45 offenders classed as psychiatrically abnormal, it was thought that at the time of the crime 21 women and 7 men were suffering from psychotic or severe neurotic depression 2 men and 2 women from schizophrenic psychoses, and that a further 2 men had acted under the influence of morbid jealousy (a very common symptom among male murderers). All of these were thought likely to have been declared insane or of diminished responsibility had they come to court. Perhaps the most doubtful among them was the case of a man with delusions of marital infidelity (Case 10, p. 81). Although most psychi-atrists are prepared to classify this type of disturbance as a paranoid illness, which involves warped emotions and judge-ment, Lord Parker, C.J., has ruled that it is not for doctors to decide whether or not a man had grounds for believing his wife unfaithful, and the appeal by the paranoid offender in question was refused.[1]

Of those classed as 'psychopaths' or 'severely neurotic or unstable' 6 were exluded from the 'insane' group. For instance, the 2 aggressive psychopaths (Cases 22 and 40) described in the section on criminal types were not considered likely candidates for a finding of 'insanity' or 'diminished responsibility'. This is admittedly a moot point, but according to Whitlock, in pleas of diminished responsibility 'aggressive psychopathy as such is a poor defence unless other factors such as epilepsy, mental defect or sexual abnormality are present in addition to the psychopathy'.[2] In the following pages, examples are taken from each of these categories of abnormality, commencing with the depressives, who were much the most frequent.

(2) Methods of Killing

In the main sample of 78 murder-suicide incidents some comparisons were made to determine whether the crimes committed by offenders ranked as presumptively 'insane' were in any way distinguishable. In the first place, females were over-represented among the 'insane' offenders of whom 24 out of 39 were women. In the 'sane' group, which also contained 39 offenders, only 10 were women. The difference was due to the inclusion in the 'insane' group of a substantial number of depressed mothers who killed their children. These same depressed mothers were also responsible for the fact that the average age of the 'insane' offenders was 40, four years younger than the average age of the rest of the offenders. (The 24 'insane' women had an average age of 36½, the 10 'sane' women offenders had an average age of 42.)

It has sometimes been suggested of murders in general that those committed by the insane are carried out with special

---

[1] R. v. Ahmed Din [1962] 2 All E.R. 124

[2] *Criminal Responsibility and Mental Illness*, p. 100. In R. v. Jennion [1962] 1 All E.R. 689, in which a woman was sentenced for murder in spite of evidence of psychopathy, it was affirmed that it is for the jury to decide the issue of diminished responsibility. In R. v. McCrorey [1962] Crim. L.R. 703, a conviction for capital murder was quashed in the case of an aggressive psychopath, liable to uncontrolled, explosive violence, who killed in furtherance of theft.

ferocity and by particularly violent methods. The Home Office investigation by Gibson and Klein did not go into this question, but some older data are available, published by Norwood East.[1] He gave figures for 500 prosecuted male murderers, comparing the methods used by those held responsible and those declared insane. His figures showed no substantial difference between the two groups. Of the methods of killing used by 200 sane male murderers, East found 31% fell into the category of stabbing or slashing; 27% into the category of battering by blows, kicks or blunt instruments; 14% were deaths by strangulation or asphyxiation, and 18% by shooting. The corresponding percentage for 300 murders by insane offenders were 43%, 21%, 10% and 19% respectively. In a more recent study of homicides by sane and insane groups of offenders in New Jersey, Gibbens[2] reached the same conclusion, that there was no substantial difference in their methods of killing.

In murders combined with suicide the methods used for killing the victims differ from those of ordinary murders because the offenders are so often women, and the victims so often children. In general, women eschew shooting and favour poisoning, and unfortunately young children fall relatively unsuspecting and unresisting victims to the lethal effects of coal gas. Considering the main sample of 78 murder-suicide offenders and taking the methods of killing used by men and women separately[3] no great difference emerged between the killings by 'sane' and 'insane' offenders, except that, of the male offenders, a large proportion of the sane murderers (one-third compared with one-sixth) used a gun. Since shooting demands a certain preparedness and skill, this difference is hardly surprising. Incidentally, the 5 negro males in the main sample all chose violent methods of killing. Four of them, motivated by sexual jealousy, attacked wives or girl-friends, two of them stabbing their victims repeatedly with extreme ferocity, two of them using no more force than necessary. The fifth man ran amok, shooting at all and sundry indiscriminately.

Apart from the method of killing, the degree of violence employed was also substantially independent of mental state. Thus, the 16 murderers in the main sample who used three or more shots, stabs, etc., to accomplish their end were equally

[1] op. cit., p. 369   [2] op. cit.   [3] See Table 15.

divided between the sane and insane groups. However, 3 murderers who used absurdly prolonged violence were all insane. One woman went on battering her husband's head with a chopper long after life was extinct (Case 77), one man strangled, battered and stabbed again and again (Case 63), and another, having stabbed his wife repeatedly, poured paraffin over her and himself and set both alight (Case 48).

(3) Depressive Offenders

In its classic, text-book variety depressive illness takes the form of recurrent attacks of irrational melancholia of such overwhelming severity as to lead to complete confusion and paralysis of mental life, to loss of sense of reality, and even to loss of appreciation of immediate surroundings. Delusions of a characteristically guilt-ridden and miserable quality may accompany the depressed mood; the sufferer may believe for example that he has committed some great sin and has no right to live, or that his insides are being eaten away by some incurable disease. Both thought and movement are slowed down, in some cases to such an extent that the patient lies helpless and speechless in a stupor, and would soon die from thirst if left untreated. In other cases, an agitated state of restless misery occurs in place of retardation or stupor. Typically, the first attack strikes in middle life, and inquiry reveals an hereditary predisposition, indicated by other members of the family similarly affected in several generations. The episodes of depression may be interspersed with occasional attacks of mania, characterized by extreme excitability, over-activity and sometimes elation. Depressive attacks usually subside spontaneously in a few months (provided always the patient has not died or killed himself) and the sufferer resumes a full and normal life. Certain drugs which have a specific action on cerebral enzymes will cut short the illness quite dramatically. This is the endogenous psychotic form of depression, so called because it appears more closely related to individual constitutional factors than to external stress, and because it produces utter mental confusion and insanity. More difficult to diagnose is the neurotic depressive reaction, a similar but less severe form of illness, which does not progress to delusions, hallucinations or other signs of outright madness, and is usually brought on by psychologically stressful events acting upon an individual of anxious, neurotic disposition.

Of the 28 offenders in the main sample who were considered to be suffering from psychiatric depression about half had the classic psychotic form of illness. In the following example, the woman's psychotic state was unmistakable. The sudden onset of desperate agitation for no apparent external reason in a previously happy and normal person, together with the family history of suicide, strongly suggested that this was an attack of endogenous depression in a constitutionally predisposed person:

Case 37
A physically healthy and very happily married young mother became suddenly agitated one night, crying out that she didn't know what was the matter with her, and that she would have to go to the madhouse. She complained of terrible headaches and behaved strangely, taking the baby out of its cot and hugging it to her in bed saying: 'I am very happy. We must make a good life for . . . .' [the baby]. Next morning she leapt out of an upper window with the baby in her arms. She had had no previous attack herself, but a near relative had also committed suicide.

Eleven of the 28 depressives had had psychiatric treatment. In those cases which were still under supervision, or had been recently in mental hospital, the evidence as to diagnosis was conclusive, as in the following case:

Case 77
A middle-aged woman, under treatment in mental hospital for involutional depression, discharged herself against medical advice. A week later she killed her husband with an axe, and after cleaning herself of his blood, she committed suicide by hanging.

She had not had any previous attack, but had been ill for some nine months, complaining of depression, inability to concentrate, and loss of sleep, weight and appetite. She became slow in speech and movement, and wandered about the house, aimless and worrying, and neglected the domestic work, although hitherto she had been over-conscientious and houseproud. She was admitted to hospital, where it was found she had classic symptoms of psychotic depression, namely delusions (that she was being poisoned and would never recover), ideas of guilt (that she was no use and ought to be put away) and hallucinations (of her dead mother's voice). She received treatment by electroplexy, which produced a temporary improvement, but she was still depressed and worried when she insisted on leaving hospital.

On returning home she appeared much worse, could not occupy herself, sat staring in front of her, and occasionally cursing her husband or accusing him (unjustifiably) of infidelity. She threatened to take her life with a knife, and on another occasion stood over her husband with a knife, but both times he was able to get the weapon away from her. Unfortunately he did not call for medical assistance because he did not want his wife committed to hospital against her will.

The murder of small children by their mothers was much the commonest type of crime among the depressive offenders, and the following example, typical of its kind, could well stand for a large section of the whole sample:

Case 16

A married woman in her early thirties gassed herself and an infant child of 4 years of age during one morning when her husband was out at work. The woman came from a poor background, both materially and psychologically. She never knew her own father, was brought up together with a large number of step-siblings, and her mother was a nervous woman who had been in a mental hospital several times. At an early age she went to live with a much older man who had parted from his own wife. They stayed together till she killed herself and their only child.

She complained of various difficulties, in particular bad housing conditions, unfriendly neighbours trying to get her to move out, sexual frigidity, and worry about having given up her religion to fit in with her 'husband'. During the year preceding her death, these difficulties took on exaggerated proportions. She worried endlessly about everything, lost her appetite and a considerable amount of weight, and complained of pains in the back and headaches. In the last six months, she refused sexual relations with her husband on the grounds that she was fearful of another pregnancy, having been frightened by a miscarriage and haemorrhage some years before. Two months before her death she took an overdose of sleeping tablets, and was admitted to hospital for washing out of the stomach. A few weeks later, having been found with her head in the gas oven, she was admitted to a mental hospital, where she was noted to be apathetic and listless, and to describe her troubles in a flat, lifeless tone of voice.

Within a week, she discharged herself against advice, and returned home because she wanted to look after her child. Visited by a psychiatric social worker, she appeared calm and self-possessed, and said she now felt able to cope with things and had no wish to try again to kill herself. Since she returned home the child had scarcely left her side, and had asked anxiously that mother would not leave again. She felt she would be all right as soon as she got into new accommodation that had been promised her. She accepted an appointment to attend a psychiatric out-patient department, although she did ask if it was compulsory.

On moving to a new flat she immediately started to complain of loneliness, although her husband tried to get her to go out and meet her new neighbours. She killed herself three days after failing to keep her clinic appointment.

The above example was rather characteristic of depressive illness, with loss of energy, appetite and weight, vague physical symptoms, and excessive rumination over difficulties (in this instance housing), but with no improvement when the reasons for complaint were removed. In the next example, because the depressive state was precipitated by bereavement, the patho-logical quality of the woman's reaction was not appreciated by those in contact with her.

Case 7

A woman in her mid-thirties, who was particularly devoted to her family, and showed a good deal of concern if ever her children were sick with ordinary childish ailments, was greatly upset by the unexpected and sudden death of her husband after years of contented married life. She was in close touch with her own relatives, who kept her company after her bereavement. It was realized that she was not in her normal state, as she made a number of distraught threats about taking her own and her children's lives. She had never before had any mental illness or suicidal tendency. In the early hours of the day of the funeral she attempted to gas herself. Later in the day, she slipped away from observation, and gave some of her sedatives to her small children. She was fortunately discovered in the act, the children were taken to hospital and successfully treated for poisoning, and then returned home. After this, she appeared more normal, expressed regret for her actions, and seemed glad to have the children back, although rather harassed by them. Then, two days after the first attempt, she rose silently in the night and cut the throats of her children and herself with a razor she had secretly purchased in the meantime.

When the most noticeable symptoms of a depressive illness take the form of an excessive preoccupation with real or imagined physical ailments, the psychiatric significance of the condition is easily missed, and this in fact appears to have happened in several of these cases. In the following example, the murderer was under psychiatric treatment as an out-patient and the incident took place in between weekly appointments:

Case 27
A middle-aged man under treatment for a slipped intervertebral lumbar disc, with which condition he had been off work for some months, complained of numerous symptoms – headaches, dizziness, neck pains, blackouts – not accounted for by his physical condition. From time to time he expressed various hypochondriacal fears, of cancer, venereal disease, paralysis and so on, for which he was eventually referred to a psychiatrist, who diagnosed a chronic anxiety state. A few days after his first interview, he murdered his wife in the night with a hammer and then hanged himself.

In the next example of depressive illness, the sufferer's morbid preoccupations revolved around the common depressive theme of the possible consequences of an old venereal infection:

Case 33
A middle-aged man, who had been to all intents and purposes happily married for nearly twenty years, was noticed by a relative to be depressed and off his food. His wife was unwell, but when it was suggested she might go into hospital he became agitated and started to cry. He seemed afraid to call a doctor, and was so depressed the relative told him he needed a doctor as much as his wife. His wife was in fact suffering from a nervous disorder.

He killed both his wife and adolescent child in carefully pre-arranged murders, and then gassed himself some hours later, having left behind notes referring to his victims in most affectionate terms and asking to be buried with them, explaining that he could not bear the shame of the disease.

He believed the disease had affected them all and that his wife was dying, and he begged forgiveness for his wickedness. He warned the police not to handle the bodies for fear of infection.

Although most clear-headed and determined in planning and executing the murders, and in the composition of the suicide notes, the murderer appeared to have done nothing at all to check whether he or his family were really infected.

More difficult to classify were some of the examples of depression of neurotic reactive type, in which stressful circumstances were clearly present, but the individual's reactions seemed out of all proportion to the realities of the situation. One had then to decide whether the ensuing behaviour could be regarded as extreme reactions in a normal person, or whether the stressful situation had precipitated an illness which, gathering its own momentum as it were, would have resulted in continued irrationality and persistent mental symptoms regardless of external realities. In the following example it was thought that a definite illness was present, and the offender was classified accordingly:

Case 6

A young married woman gassed herself and her small child. She had been seen by a psychiatrist a few months previously, following a suicidal attempt with sleeping tablets. On that occasion, the attempt had followed a quarrel with her husband about his association with a woman at work. Neither the psychiatrist nor the family doctor considered it at all likely that the husband intended to desert or have a serious extra-marital affair, and the wife's suicidal bid was thought to have been more demonstrative than resolute.

Following this episode, the wife avoided further discussion with the doctors, but she remained far from well. Her husband reported that she slept poorly and was losing weight. She had always been anxious and highly strung, subject to depressed moods, and dependent upon heavy smoking and a certain amount of drinking. Although she was still able to conceal these symptoms from outsiders, the husband realized she was getting worse, so much so that he asked a relative to have one of their children to stay for a time as his wife might have to go into hospital again. It was while he was away depositing this child that the wife killed herself and the other child.

In the above example, in spite of the presence of some rational concern about the husband's philandering, the wife's reactions were disproportionate both in quality and degree.

Although in reality her husband did his best to prove her fears groundless, she got steadily worse. This sequence of events is not uncommon in depressive illness. The patient rationalizes the depressive mood changes attributing them to some objective worry. Only at a later stage, when the agitation and depression have become utterly disproportionate to the supposed cause, and the removal of the worrying circumstances brings no relief, do the relatives realize that the patient has been mentally ill all the time. In one such case known to the writer, a middle-aged married woman with a large, ugly nose became increasingly sensitive and miserable about her appearance. Although seen by a psychiatrist who advised treatment for depression, she refused and insisted that all her troubles arose from her disfigurement. She underwent a successful plastic operation, in which her nose was broken and re-set. After this, her pre-occupation transferred from the shape of the nose to the redness caused by recent surgery, and she became so distressed that she made an attempt on her life. Finally treatment by electro-plexy was accepted, and she reverted to her former cheerful efficient self.

In classifying some of these murder-suicide offenders the distinction between a 'pathological' reaction and a 'normal' reaction of grief or despair was hard to make and sometimes almost arbitrary. A normal grief response is supposed to be short-lived, closely tied to an actual life situation, and characterized by depressed mood without other complicating symptoms. It is certainly arguable that some of the offenders previously described as 'relatively normal' were in fact passing through a neurotic phase at the time of their crime. Case 15 (p. 48), the old man who was far from well at the time he decided that he and his wife should die together, and Case 5 (p. 49), the man with an inoperable cancer who decided that he would not leave his aged mother to die alone, were both suffering from organic diseases liable to precipitate reactive depression. For present purposes, however, the label 'depressive illness' was limited to those offenders who showed recognizably abnormal or irrational responses, and excluded the milder forms of neurotic reaction. In the following example, which was one of the more difficult to classify, the offender was not in fact placed with those suffering from a severe depressive illness.

It appears she was driven to a state of desperation by circumstances with which she was temperamentally unfitted to cope:

Case 28

A middle-aged woman was made very unhappy by her husband's persistent infidelity and by his violent tempers during which he often struck and threatened her. He was considerably younger. She made numerous complaints about him to relatives and others, saying that he had on more than one occasion tried to murder her, but it would appear that her allegations were greatly exaggerated. She believed that other women had put him against her and were persuading him to get rid of her. After writing a long note to the effect that she and her husband had decided to die together, she shot him from behind and then killed herself.

In contrast, the following example was in fact included among the cases of depressive illness because the offender's symptoms were conspicuous and persistent and out of her normal character:

Case 31

An elderly woman, previously active and sociable became very depressed and seclusive following a paralysing 'stroke' sustained by her husband, to whom she was very devoted. She dreaded her husband's death, and for a year or more she spoke so frequently of suicide and 'dying together' that relatives ceased to take her seriously. Although wealthy, she became so depressed she neglected to buy food and fuel. Finally, the couple were found dead from gas poisoning. Medical investigation showed that the old man had had a recent coronary thrombosis and that there was some possibility that his wife may have thought him dead when she turned on the gas taps.

The following case, which was also very difficult to classify, was finally included among those offenders considered to be suffering from a definite depressive illness. The chief evidence was the opinion of the family doctor, who knew the offender and his circumstances well. The case presented another instance in which exhaustion and serious organic disease played an important part:

Case 68

An elderly married man, well respected and known to have been devoted to his wife for forty years, murdered her and killed himself almost immediately afterwards. The general practitioner diagnosed a psychiatric depression of 'reactive' type, brought on by the strain of family troubles and his own poor health. Owing to the serious illness of other members of the family, he and his wife, who was also in indifferent health, had had to look after some small children, a task which he found extremely burdensome. The murderer himself was seriously ill, having not fully recovered from an operation for prostatectomy. He was unable to sleep and rather obviously depressed. The post-mortem showed a recurrence of the cancerous growth in the prostatic region, as well as signs of serious heart disease – advanced coronary atheroma with recent thrombosis – so that he could not have had long to live.

In this final example, which was classified only after much difficulty as an instance of severe neurotic depression, there were obvious external stresses in the form of marital disharmony, but these were themselves the product of the wife's neurotic inability (presumably based upon unresolved oedipal fixation) to sustain a relationship with a man of her own age.

Case 23
A young married woman had been under treatment for some time from her family doctor for what was described as a depressive state, which manifested in anxiety, depression and irritability, and in severe headaches. She was a more intelligent and dominating personality than her husband, with whom she got on very badly. He was in the forces, and for some years they had been having frequent quarrels. She had broken off sexual relations and discouraged him from spending his leaves at home. In contrast to her coldness towards her husband, she was on particularly close terms with her father-in-law, paid him a lot of attention, and went out for walks in his company. In fact her behaviour in this respect provoked an outburst of temper on the part of her mother-in-law. Immediately after this scene, when her husband was due to arrive, she put him off when he telephoned, and then killed herself and her small children with gas. She had previously been regarded as a particularly proud and devoted mother.

(4) *Schizophrenic Offenders*
Characteristically, the most prominent symptoms of schizophrenia consist of peculiar, muddled thinking, bizarre preoccupations and delusions, and a mood of flat apathetic

detachment from surrounding realities. Violence is not typical of the average patient. The commonest emotional display is fatuous giggling, incongruous with the actual situation. However, excitability and violence do occur in this illness, and the catatonic schizophrenic, longtime mute and statuesque in a corner, who suddenly breaks out into murderous *furor* and attacks some unsuspecting bystander, is well known in clinical tradition. Similarly, patients who run amok, attacking all and sundry, are likely to be schizophrenics. But such events happen very rarely. Insanely twisted though they are, the motives in most schizophrenic murders are fairly readily discernible. Thus the paranoid schizophrenic who attacks his imagined persecutors; the young male, preoccupied with incest fantasies on the Freudian pattern, who commits matricide; or the deluded husband who kills his wife after misinterpreting her cough as a signal to a supposed lover, are all displaying understandable though crazy behaviour. The effect of the schizophrenic illness is to weaken restraint and so to allow some quite trivial stimulus to trigger off violent and uninhibited expression of the individual's underlying conflicts and latent aggression. The main peculiarity of schizophrenics has little to do with the psychopathology of their aggression – which conforms to the usual themes – but consists of an inability to test their thoughts against reality, with the consequence that fantasy and suspicion may be translated directly into disastrous action. As with the psychotic depressive, a murderous outburst may bring temporary calm and relief to the schizophrenic, but the general course of the illness remains unaltered, the patient soon fastens his attention upon other pretexts for resentment, and another round of delusions begins.

Apart from the minority of so-called schizo-affective disorders, in which pronounced mood swings complicate the picture, schizophrenic illness rarely leads to suicide. Consequently, although this diagnosis is commonly made on insane murderers generally, one would not at first sight expect many murder-suicide crimes to be committed by schizophrenics, unless, for some reason, homicidal schizophrenics are in this respect untypical. Jonathan Gould remarks that in a series of Broadmoor patients examined by him, the only two who committed suicide in hospital (both a considerable time after he had ceased seeing them) were schizophrenics, not depressives.[1]

The results of some American studies of murderers suggest that the combination of homicidal and suicidal tendencies is not uncommon in schizophrenic offenders. In a clinical review of some psychotic patients admitted to Bellevue Hospital, New York, after murdering their own children, Lauretta Bender found that most of them were women suffering from schizophrenia.[2] The natural psychological mechanism of identification, which makes a mother feel her child as a part of herself, was carried to dangerous extremes by these psychotic mothers. They tended to project their own symptoms into their child until it became as much a focus of hypochondrical fears or delusions as the organs of their own body. One such mother, after killing her child Kenneth, explained 'I could hear them say that I was losing my mind . . . I thought that Kenneth was changing too. I could see it. His eyes changed the same way mine changed.' At first this unfortunate mother sought release in attempted suicide, then she attempted to kill both herself and the child, and finally she killed only the child, after which her own mental symptoms subsided to some extent. In another instance, a woman of suspicious, jealous and irritable disposition fell ill with schizophrenia and developed paranoid delusions of persecution by a gang that she believed was following her around. One day her apartment caught fire, but when people came to her assistance she misinterpreted the situation and attempted to throw herself and her children into the street below to escape from her supposed persecutors. She and one of her children were forcibly pulled back, but her baby fell and was killed. In this case, the woman's close identification with her children meant that they were involved in the unreal but dangerous situations created by her paranoid delusions.

Perhaps too much concentration upon the well-known altruistic theme of depressive homicide may have obscured the role of other serious mental disturbances, notably paranoia

[1] 'The Psychiatry of Major Crime,' *Recent Progress in Psychiatry*, 1959, p. 325
[2] 'Psychiatric Mechanisms in Child Murderers,' *Jour. Nervous and Mental Diseases*, 1934

and psychopathy, in releasing the indiscriminate aggression that leads to various combinations of murder and suicide. That the unrestrained rage of the psychopath may sometimes lead to 'murder and suicide from motives the very opposite of altruistic was well illustrated by a case reported by Neiberg.[1] A young man with definite aggressive, psychopathic traits shot his girl-friend and later killed himself in prison. His aggressive nature, and also his tendency to turn his rage against himself, had been displayed clearly, even at the age of 12, when, following a quarrel with his mother about her intention to send him to a Hebrew school, he made a suicidal attempt by swallowing iodine. His violent behaviour and disobedience at home were later followed by insubordination and absence without leave during his career in the forces. Only a few months before the murder, he had had a violent outburst in a public bar. Due to his reckless driving he had a car accident in which the girl he wanted to marry was injured. By agreement with her family, the marriage was delayed so she could sue him for damages which would presumably be covered by insurance. He became enraged by the length of the delay, and while in a desperate mood he shot and killed the girl. He said that at the time of the crime he was thinking that he might be sent to the electric chair and hoping that it would happen. Following the shooting he made several attempts at suicide, and at his trial he insisted that he had killed intentionally and wanted no mercy. After sentence of death had been passed, but when commutation seemed likely, he finally succeeded in hanging himself.

This case provides an unusually clear example of the aggressively ambivalent relationship described by Freud as the typical precursor of depression and suicide; at the same time it demonstrates that such mental processes are not necessarily restricted to classical forms of neurotic or psychotic depression.

In point of fact, the main sample of 78 murder-suicides included only 3 schizophrenic offenders. This scarcity of schizophrenics in comparison with the large number of depressives is consistent with English clinical experience which suggests that among schizophrenic patients, especially those with paranoid delusions, aggressive outbursts against others

[1] 'Murder and Suicide,' *Archiv. Criminal Psychodynamics*, 1961

are much commoner than suicidal attempts. All three schizophrenics showed unusually violent fluctuations of mood. In two of them the disturbance was more like schizo-affective psychosis – a mixture of both depressive and schizophrenic symptoms. In other words, even the few schizophrenic cases which were present did not run true to form, but had a noticeable admixture of depressive features, as in the following example:

Case 48
A young coloured man murdered his wife and killed himself in an incident of extreme violence. His own death might possibly have been unintentional, and an open verdict was returned at the inquest instead of the usual one of death by suicide.

Six weeks previously while out with a friend he had 'collapsed' on the floor and been taken to a hospital casualty department where he lay stiff and inert. He was diagnosed as a hysteric, and revived with stimulants, after which he appeared well, and was discharged. Later that same day, having travelled a long distance by train, he again 'collapsed' in the street and was admitted to hospital, where he was found to be psychotic. He was vague, confused and unco-operative on examination and it was impossible to establish contact with him. He attacked nurses and walked about the ward naked. During his ten days' stay in hospital he changed from being largely inert and uncommunicative to a state of elation and over-activity. He gave no clear account of himself, and although he wrote a letter addressed to his wife he denied that she was his wife. From subsequent inquiries it appears she had in fact left him temporarily because he shut himself away, refusing to talk to her, saying that he was studying for an examination. The hospital authorities made a tentative diagnosis of schizophrenia.

He was taken from hospital by a relative, after which he behaved quite normally and went back to live with his wife. Four weeks later he was saying his wife was pregnant by another man. The subsequent post-mortem showed she was not pregnant. According to a neighbour's testimony, he was a violent-tempered and excitable man who always shouted at his wife. One morning, during the early hours, he was observed going into the garden, dressed all in white, where he dug a trench and buried some tiles. When dying, he made various confused remarks, several of which were to the effect that life was not worth living and he wanted to die.

Although regarded as an instance of schizophrenia, the case just quoted had a number of unusual features, chief of which was the rapid alternation between phases of apparent normality and of complete psychotic collapse. The curious ritual in the garden sounded like florid schizophrenic behaviour, although the rapid change from mutism and inertia to elation and over-activity resembled more the symptoms of manic depressive psychosis, as did the death wishes voiced after the murder.

The following example was more typical of paranoid schizophrenia, although again the depressive emotional disturbance was quite pronounced, in contrast to the apathy and flattening of emotion which is the more usual symptom of this illness:

Case 25

A middle-aged married woman was admitted to mental hospital following a suicidal gesture in which she made some attempt to gas herself and her small child. She was found to have persecutory delusions and hallucinations. She believed that everyone was talking about an act of marital infidelity in her past, she could hear neighbours' voices talking through the walls and she saw elaborate hidden meanings in the most casual comments. Under observation, she revealed still more fantastic delusions, for instance that she was suffering the effects of a witch hunt for communists, that there was a plot afoot to murder the royal family, and that rays emanated from the television which were harmful to herself and her child. While in hospital she secreted some tablets and swallowed them putting herself into a coma from which she was revived with some difficulty. She explained that she could not bear to see her child suffer persecution by 'rays'.

After nearly six months in hospital she appeared quite well again and was discharged. A relative of hers had had a similar illness some years before, and partially recovered, although still 'a bit odd and suspicious'. On returning home to her husband and child she seemed quite well for a few months, when her persecutory delusions returned and she had what her husband described as 'periodic bouts of depression' of varying duration and severity. One day, while he was out at work, she finally killed herself and the child in the manner she had attempted fourteen months previously.

In the third example of schizophrenia, the information available was scanty, but the paranoid element was plain enough:

Case 69
A middle-aged widow, living alone with one child, killed herself and the child with gas. It appears she was preoccupied with an old love affair, and she left behind a complaining note addressed to the man concerned.

She had not been in hospital, and her doctor did not know her very well, so her mental state can only be inferred. She was known to have been mentally disturbed for some years, she made no friends, and people noticed her talking to herself whilst walking along in the street. The police reported that she suffered from hallucinations and that she had complained to them of imaginary detectives following her about. She planned the suicide carefully, sending off in advance a note about the disposition of her possessions, and cancelling the usual deliveries at her house.

One cannot generalize with safety from only three cases, but the fact that all three showed marked depressive reactions in conjunction with paranoid delusions does bear out a suggestion that might have been predicted on clinical grounds, namely that the greatest risk of homicide-suicide would occur in paranoids whose aggressive emotions are not yet blunted by schizophrenic apathy, and especially in those in whom the emotional distress takes a depressive form.

(5) *Morbid Jealousy*
In the main sample of murder-suicide, two offenders were classified as suffering from morbid jealousy. Whether this can be regarded as an illness in itself, or whether such persons should be regarded under the headings of either schizophrenia or psychopathy, is open to argument. In practice, in some male patients, jealousy amounts to a monomania and may be present in extremely irrational forms, without signs of schizophrenic disorder of thinking in other respects, and without the generalized impulsiveness and lack of social conscience of the typical psychopath. Such was the case in the following example:

Case 10
A young married couple were found gassed in bed. The wife having died first, it appeared plausible that the husband had waited till she was asleep and then turned on the gas.

It transpired that the husband had been insanely jealous towards his wife, keeping her and their child almost like prisoners in the house, accusing her of infidelities with acquaintances, and treating her with such violence that on one occasion she left him and went to the police for protection. His violent and suspicious temperament also showed itself when their child fell ill, and at first he would not allow a doctor to be called, and later made a scene at the hospital to prevent the child receiving an injection. He left behind a vindictive suicide note accusing a man-friend of being responsible for their deaths and at the same time specifying some crimes the friend had committed. Subsequent police inquiries established that the allegations were without foundation.

The coroner stated that the offender was undoubtedly unstable and mentally unbalanced. He had had to have psychiatric treatment when in the services.

In the second case of morbid jealousy, a daughter was killed by her father:

Case 61
The victim, a woman in her thirties, was mentally subnormal. Ordinarily, she was quiet and docile and lived a very isolated life but recently she had been referred to a psychiatric clinic on account of obstinate behaviour. She had been dismissed from work for laughing inappropriately and showing a 'couldn't-t-care-less' attitude. The precipitating factor appeared to be a severe conflict with her father who was described as a quiet man, and 'wrapped up in his daughter to the point of obsession'. He was extremely emotional about her association with a man-friend. She refused to listen and became defiant and insolent. He had gone so far as to comment that he would see her dead before going with the man. He was sufficiently upset by the situation to visit his doctor complaining of nervous depression. The doctor felt he would probably have reacted similarly to any other man the daughter had chosen.

One day force of circumstances had left the two of them alone in the house. It appears the daughter dressed in preparation for going out against her father's wishes, whereupon he killed her impulsively and then committed suicide.

(6) *Aggressive Psychopaths*

At least four of the 78 murder-suicide offenders could fairly be described as aggressive psychopaths. Two (Cases 22 and 40) were cited in the discussion of offenders with a criminal record.[1] Unlike these, the following case was placed in the 'insane' group, since the paranoid ideas were so prominent that a jury would probably have given him the benefit of the doubt on the issue of responsibility. Unfortunately, no medical information was available in his case, so his mental state remains largely a matter of conjecture:

Case 20
An unmarried man, lodging with his parents, was recognized by his relatives to be embittered and unconfiding, but was not considered by them to be actually mad. During army service he had sustained a slight injury after which he complained of severe symptoms. When the doctors did not take the matter very seriously, he slashed himself to draw attention to the grievance, and was subsequently discharged, after which he spent a lot of time petitioning various authorities for a pension for his supposed disability.

He seems to have been a man of violent temperament, having been discharged from one job after striking a woman in the face, and having had various quarrels and fights with work-mates. Shortly before his death he wrote an abusive note to the effect that he was fed up and in pain and was going to end his own life and also those of the people he hated. He then went to visit several people, a former work-mate, a man who owed him money, and a former neighbour with whom he had had a quarrel, and shot them all (one of them died), afterwards killing himself. His grievances against two of the victims were insubstantial, if not entirely imaginary.

The following case was also deemed to fall into the 'insane' or non-responsible category on account of psychiatric evidence as to his history of mental disturbance:

Case 57
The offender was an excitable, talkative, boastful man of low intelligence. He was constantly unemployed on account of symptoms of backache, which were considered by hospital doctors to be largely hysterical. He was referred to a psychiatrist and put on a tranquillizer. He was in severe conflict with his wife, and various authorities had been approached to intervene on account of his violence towards her and his children. He was

---

[1] See Chapter vi.

described by a family doctor as 'a pale little man, full of resentments against the world and immensely aggressive'. He so resented interference that when his baby had pneumonia he turned out of the house the doctor who called to examine the child. He was reported to have been so irritated by his baby crying during a fatal illness that he picked it up and threw it across the room. His wife had been seen by social workers badly bruised and with a tooth knocked out following arguments with her husband, and on another occasion he had attacked his wife in a very frightening way in the presence of a social worker who had called about the children.

Six weeks before the murder, the offender's wife finally left the home, and two children remained behind. He made numerous threats that unless she returned he would kill the children and himself. Finally he did so, leaving behind a note blaming his wife.

(7) *Markedly Neurotic or Unstable Offenders*

The 5 men and 2 women classified under this heading all had persistent and pronounced disorders of personality, most of them being chronically moody or aggressive, and all of them being quite severely disabled in their capacity to maintain ordinary human relationships. Some of the offenders previously described as 'relatively normal' showed unmistakably neurotic reactions. For instance, in Case 54 (p. 51), the student who was unable to withstand the strain of examinations; in Case 13 (p. 50) and Case 28 (p. 74), both women enmeshed in marital problems partly of their own making, and in Case 72 (p. 53), the man who got into debt and saw no solution, the offenders' troubles were in each instance aggravated by their own neurotic predisposition. In these cases, however, their neurosis was a relatively circumscribed disturbance, manifest only under particular circumstances of stress. This type of reaction, being extremely common, was not such as to earn for the individuals in question a general reputation for mental abnormality. In contrast, in this group of 'markedly neurotic or unstable offenders' the peculiarities were such as to stand out quite clearly to the eyes of their friends or relatives. Several of these cases have already been mentioned, namely Case 58 (p. 61), the petty criminal of inadequate personality who sought refuge in alcohol and then became violent; Case 38 (p. 19), the rigid, self-absorbed, hypochondriacal spinster whose imaginary troubles made her existence unbearable; and Case 70 (p. 23), the aggressive woman of paranoid personality who refused to accept psychiatric help.

Uncontrolled aggression was the chief feature in at least four of these cases. For instance, in the following example, there was a long history of aggressive behaviour on the offender's part, but this was limited to the domestic scene, and ordinarily he would not have been classed as an aggressive psychopath:

Case 14
A middle-aged man, married nearly thirty years, was a steady worker, had never been involved in criminal offences, and was generally regarded as quite normal mentally. However, he had always been moody and violent towards his wife, and they had been separated on two occasions, under a Court Order, issued on the grounds of his cruelty. The couple were well known to the local probation officer, and appeared temperamentally incompatible. Despite continuous disputes and mutual recriminations, often arising from his practice of keeping his wife short of money and his resentment when she bought herself clothes, the wife kept returning to the marital home. Their older children left home as soon as possible to get away from the unhappy atmosphere. The man had made a number of suicidal threats, and on one occasion five years previous made an actual attempt with tablets.

They had been sleeping apart for a year, and matters reached a climax when he threatened her with a hammer and she left to go to one of her married children. She called back for the younger children, but he would not let her take them. He told her he was going to kill himself, and said the same to some relatives. A day or so later he did so gassing both himself and the children. He left behind a long letter to his wife, written in a most vindictive tone, and blaming her for their deaths. In the course of this letter he remarked upon his failing health which meant he could not carry on under the conditions she was making him live. In fact, he was under treatment for chronic heart disease, which was far advanced, and he had had a number of attacks of asthma, which were probably the result of heart failure.

The above example illustrates rather well the neurotic love-hate relationship described by the psycho-analysts, with aggression coming to a head and turning against the self when the object of ambivalent attachment is lost. The combination of desperation and vindictiveness was well known in the offender's reaction to failing health, which was felt as yet another intolerable burden for which the hated wife was to blame.

In the next example, a long period of conflict and mutual recriminations between offender and victim preceded the crime, although in his other relationships the offender would have been classed as nervous and inhibited more than aggressive:

Case 36

A middle-aged single man had suffered all his life from 'bad nerves' and had an hysterical aphonia which at times caused him to communicate in whispers although at other times he spoke normally. He had been a life-long, solitary misfit, always over-anxious and tortured by ideas of inferiority, and unable to find himself a wife, though he very much wanted to marry. He had a mental breakdown when a widow to whom he was attached remarried someone else. He agreed to enter a mental hospital, but quickly discharged himself against advice without being in any way improved. He repeated this sequence three times in quick succession. The doctors assessed him as an hysterical personality, unable to face up to his problems or co-operate in psychotherapy, who was suffering from anxiety and depression. He returned to his parental home, where he was living on uneasy terms with his step-mother. Two months later he was even more miserable and irritable than before, and apparently on impulse he attacked his step-mother, killed her, and then committed suicide.

The group of markedly unstable offenders included two more cases not so far mentioned. One of these (Case 76) was a murder committed by a work-shy alcoholic man who was still living in the parental home at a mature age. He regularly became sullen and irritable after drinking. When his own fecklessness had led to his married brother being invited to come to live in the house to help maintain the place, he developed a marked jealousy, which finally led to a shooting scene in which he killed his brother, wounded his sister-in-law, and then committed suicide.

The last of these cases was a murder of a prostitute by a chronically unstable man who had had a leucotomy:

Case 60

A chronically depressed single man, a foreign refugee in his early forties, had been in hospital several times for investigation of numerous hypochondriacal complaints. No physical cause was ever discovered. Several other members of the family had had mental illnesses. He proved a difficult, moody and unco-operative patient, but he did respond temporarily to a course of electroplexy. After various relapses, he finally underwent a leucotomy operation (bilateral orbital undercutting) following which he ceased to be so preoccupied and upset by his physical symptoms.

He subsequently formed a forlorn attachment to a prostitute, on whom he spent a lot of money. He then became jealous, asserting bitterly that she had wanted him only for money. At the time he was still complaining of insomnia, nightmares, and various aches and pains of nervous origin, for which he was having sedatives from a local doctor. During one night when they were together he strangled this woman and then killed himself with an overdose of drugs, lying down to die beside her. He left behind notes expressing his resentment against her for spurning him, and his inability to face life without her.

(8) *Insane Murder-Suicide Offenders compared with Insane Murderers brought to Trial*

Contrary to expectation, the numbers of murder-suicide offenders thought to be sufficiently abnormal to rank with legally insane or diminished responsibility offenders was not much more than in the sample of ordinary murders. The figures were 50% and 47% respectively for the main murder-suicide sample and the comparative murder sample.

It appears that throughout this century the proportion of insane among those brought to trial has remained at a remarkably constant level of a little less than half. Hopwood quotes Sir Edward Troup of the Home Office as stating: 'In the 22 years from 1901 to 1922, out of 1,445 persons committed for trial on charges of murder, 585 were convicted and 517 were found to be insane, either before trial or by special verdict of the jury, and of those convicted 13 were found insane on the Home Office inquiry.'[1] Grunhut also pointed out that in more recent decades the proportion found insane has remained at about 44% of those charged with murder.[2] The more recent Home Office research showed that since the introduction of the Homicide Act, 1957, inclusion with the insane of the new

---

[1] 'Child Murder and Insanity,' *Journ. Mental Science*, 1927
[2] op. cit.

category of 'diminished responsibility' keeps the proportion of mentally abnormal cases at 46% of those charged, or about 48% of those actually committed for trial.[1] Prior to 1957 virtually the whole of this 46% went to a mental hospital, some being found insane on arraignment and not fit to plead, some being found by jury 'guilty but insane', and some being certified insane whilst in prison serving sentence or awaiting execution. Nowadays, those found to be of diminished responsibility by virtue of their abnormality of mind are more often sent to prison than committed to Broadmoor or other mental hospitals.[2]

In the types of abnormality encountered, however, the murder-suicide and murder offenders differ very substantially, especially so in the males. Unfortunately, precise figures relating to the psychiatric conditions of insane murderers are hard to find. In the days when they all went to Broadmoor, Norwood East reported on the diagnoses made on 300 consecutive admissions of murderers.[3] From his descriptions it appears that 110 were suffering from illnesses which we should today call manic-depressive psychosis, and 94 from delusional insanity, presumably approximately equivalent to schizophrenia. More recent work suggests that most insane murderers are schizophrenic, so perhaps the position has somewhat changed.

Gould, in a survey of the admissions to Broadmoor Hospital in the years 1954–5, records that 27% carried a diagnosis of manic depressive or depressive illness, and 57% were schizophrenic or paranoid. Although a half of these admissions were murderers, the picture might have been different if other offenders had been excluded.[4] Christie, medical officer at

---

[1] op. cit., Table 7, p. 10, and *Criminal Statistics* for 1957–60

[2] R. F. Sparks, in a survey of the working of the Homicide Act in this connection, pointed out that out of 150 sentences imposed in 'diminished responsibility' cases in the years 1957 to 1962, 104 were sentences of imprisonment, either for nominal life or for fixed terms. Although the Home Secretary has the power to transfer such prisoners to a mental hospital or special mental hospital, this is not usually done, and in any case it would seem that on recovery patients so transferred are liable to be returned to prison.

[3] op. cit., p. 378 (1936)

[4] op. cit.

Winchester Prison, surveying an unselected series of 258 male homicides which he had examined (all of whom were later found insane at trial or else subsequently certified insane) noted a 20% incidence of manic depressive psychosis. A 'high percentage' of these crimes were followed by an attempt at suicide.[1]

Whatever the exact incidence may be, it is clear that depressive psychosis remains a very common diagnosis among insane English murderers, but that it is nothing like so common as among murder-suicide offenders, where this diagnosis applies to the majority of the insane cases.

Various American surveys of insane homicides have been published, and it is of some interest to see how far the contrasts found here between suicidal murderers and ordinary murderers also apply in that country. In the first place, American surveys regularly report overall a much larger proportion of schizophrenics and a much smaller proportion of melancholics among their abnormal murderers. J. W. Mohr, quoting a recent analysis of inmates of the Oakridge Unit for the criminal insane in Ontario, Canada, states that out of 73 patients who had committed or attempted homicide more than half were schizophrenic, and mostly suffering from paranoid schizophrenia, whereas only 6 had depressive psychosis.[2] Lanzkron, in a survey at Matteawan State Hospital, New York, covering the years 1956 to 1961, found that of 150 consecutive admissions of charged or indicted murderers, who were committed on account of present insanity, 93 were diagnosed as suffering from schizophrenia and paranoid psychosis, 14 from other kinds of psychosis, 34 from psychopathy, and only 9 from depressive psychosis. As regards operative motives, paranoid delusions figured in 56 cases, morbid jealousy or delusions of infidelity in 30 cases, and depressive ideas in only 17. Attempted suicide was not mentioned.[3] Similar findings were reported by Gibbens in a documentary study of abnormal murderers, based on a series of consecutive admissions to the State Hospital of New Jersey. The condition present at the time of the crime

[1] 'The Manic Depressive Psychoses in relation to Crime,' *Medico-Legal Jour.*, 1942
[2] 'Prison or Hospital,' *Canadian Psychiatric Assn. Jour.*, 1964
[3] 'Murder and Insanity,' *Amer. Journ. Psychiatry*, 1963

(in a total of 68 cases) was most frequently schizophrenia or 'paranoid condition' (49%), and less often depression (13%). The remainder consisted for the most part of miscellaneous organic conditions, e.g. epilepsy, G.P.I., arterio-sclerosis, alcoholic deterioration (28%).[1]

Gibbens pointed out that successful suicide following homicide was remarkably rare in New Jersey. However, out of a total of 115 homicides who were either insane when they committed the crime or became so later, 14 made suicidal attempts at the time of the killing, and a further 18 made suicidal attempts later. In a similar-sized group of comparable homicides by sane persons Gibbens found that only 7 made suicidal attempts. Somewhat similar findings were reported in New York in an earlier psychiatric study of homicide cases by McDermaid and Winkler.[2] Of 16 non-psychotic murderers, 4 showed some suicidal tendencies and one of these made a serious suicidal attempt during trial. Among 11 psychotic murderers, however, 'suicidal tendencies were much more pronounced' and 5 offenders actually attempted suicide. Most of these suicidal psychotics were considered schizophrenic. One 30-year-old negro man, for instance, had delusions of being hounded by persecutors who followed him in the street, and he also described hallucinatory 'voices' telling him to kill himself or else he might be killed by someone else. In fact he did make a suicidal attempt which led to his admission to hospital. A year later he committed murder, shooting dead a woman who had refused his amorous advances. In another instance a young housewife, who was unhappily married to a violent tempered and neglectful husband, was treated in a state hospital for schizophrenia. A year after her release from hospital, following an argument with her husband, she made a suicidal attempt with gas. She was rescued, but her 4-year-old child who was with her died. On examination she was evasive, suspicious and irritable. Two years later, still in hospital, she showed further mental deterioration, with regressive symptoms, and the diagnosis of schizophrenia was confirmed.

These American findings present some difficulty in interpretation in terms of the situation in England. Especially

[1] op. cit.

[2] *Journ. Clinical Psychopathology*, 1950

puzzling was the observation that suicidal murderers in America were usually schizophrenics and not depressives. Perhaps some of the American suicidal murderers would have been considered 'depressives' if examined in England, being counted as 'schizophrenics' in these studies on account of the comparatively free use of that label in American psychiatry. But variation in diagnostic conventions would not explain the relatively low incidence of suicide following murder in the United States, which applies to both sane and insane offenders. Since the number of murders in the United States is so much greater than in England, the same incidence of homicidal depressives relative to the size of the population would represent a very small percentage of the total of American homicide. On the assumption that melancholic thinking is relatively immune from cultural determinants, but that schizophrenics may sometimes reflect in morbidly exaggerated form the violent tendencies prevalent in certain sections of the community, the preponderance of schizophrenics among American psychotic murderers would be an understandable concomitant of the higher murder rate in America. However this may be, English and American findings on the connections between psychotic illness and murder do present some surprising contrasts. For instance, Gibbens pointed out that in New Jersey almost as many murderers develop their psychosis after the crime – anything from a month to ten years after – as were psychotic when they committed it.[1] It is true that in England murderers sometimes show their first signs of psychosis in prison after conviction, suggesting that the crime may have been the first symptom of illness, but this sequence is relatively uncommon. The American finding that the combination of murder and suicidal tendency is more frequent among insane than sane offenders was not replicated in our English samples. On the other hand, the prevalence of schizophrenia and psychopathy among mentally abnormal American murderers might mean that their suicidal tendencies are less extreme, and their suicidal attempts less determined and less often successful than is the case with English murderers who were more predominantly melancholic.

[1] op. cit.

VIII

The Psychology of Murder-Suicide
during Melancholia

(1) *The Altruistic Interpretation*

MOST criminological writers appear to have been aware of the importance of depressive illness in murder, and to have attributed such cases to misguided altruism. For example, the Australian authorities Wily and Stallworthy, in their treatise *Mental Abnormality and the Law* (1962), state that in their experience depressive psychosis is by far the commonest psychiatric cause of homicide and describe the typical thought process in such crimes as follows: 'From thoughts of self-destruction because life is so hopeless, and the world so wretched, it is a short step to thinking that duty demands that those normally loved most should also be taken out of the wicked world.' The Danish criminologist, Professor Hurwitz, remarks in his text-book 'Of special criminalistic interest are the *psychogenic depressions* that in extreme cases lead to family murder according to the type of "extended suicide".'[1] Similarly, Norwood East, in his early book, *Forensic Psychiatry in the Criminal Courts* (1927), remarks: 'Homicidal and suicidal impulses frequently co-exist in melancholia, and the majority of homicidal attacks are made upon members of the subject's family for whom he has a real affection.'[2] In illustration of this East quotes, among others, the case of a man who had had three attacks of depression, always accompanied by suicidal ideas, in the last of which he killed his wife and then made a determined attempt on his own life. Although financially secure, he laboured under the delusion that he was an utter

[1] *Criminology* (trans. London, 1952), p. 158
[2] p. 332

failure and unable to provide for his wife in future. Hallucinatory voices urged him to put an end to both their miseries.
There seemed no reason to doubt the genuineness of his devotion
to his wife or the altruistic quality of his insane motives. F. A.
Whitlock, in a recent treatise on *Criminal Responsibility and
Mental Illness* (1963), comments: 'Severe depressive states in
which the accused kills his or her children, believing that
unless this is done some dreadful fate awaits them, are not
uncommon.'[1]

Similar views of the motivation of murders by melancholics
have been shared by most forensic experts. W. C. Sullivan
quoted as most typical the example of a melancholic man with
hypochondriacal delusions who left the place where he was
being looked after to call on his wife and cut her throat. He
told the police he knew he was dying himself and he did not
wish to leave her to face the world alone.[2]

In England, at least, this kind of delusional thinking has
been held responsible for most murders of small children by
their mothers. In a review of the cases of 253 women admitted
to Broadmoor following murderous attacks on their infants –
which most often took place during the period of lactation –
J. Baker noted that the form of insanity on admission was
almost invariably melancholia and that: 'suicide completed,
attempted, or contemplated, almost invariably accompanies
the infanticide.[3] Their act, although at first sight it looks like
infanticide, followed by suicide, is in reality, so to speak, only
the completion of their own self-inflicted death. To die alone
and leave their children is impossbile for them, the children
being an organic part of themselves.' In a later review, J. S.
Hopwood surveyed the cases of the 166 women who were
admitted to Broadmoor during the first 25 years of this century
following charges of child murder committed during the
lactation period. He found definite suicidal ideas present in
98 cases, of whom 59 had made actual attempts on their lives.[4]
This view was further confirmed by J. H. Morton in a survey
of women murderers examined at Holloway Prison.[5] In

[1] p. 28
[2] *Crime and Insanity* (London, 1924)
[3] 'Female Criminal Lunatics,' *Journ. Mental Science*, 1920
[4] op. cit.   [5] 'Female Homicides,' *Journ. Mental Science*, 1934

practically all murders of infants the underlying principle was a desire to save the victim from what was considered a worse fate. Except for the women who killed their unwanted babies when newly born, Morton found that nearly all mothers who killed their children had a family history of insanity and showed clear indications of depressive illness at the time of the crime, the chief symptoms being confusion, sleeplessness, retardation, delusions of unworthiness and depressed mood. Frequently the prisoners had attempted suicide after the murder, and others had left notes showing clearly that they had been contemplating suicide even though they made no actual attempt.

In the main sample of murder-suicides, the majority of the killings by melancholics, and especially in the cases of sacrifices of children by depressed mothers, manifestly hostile motives towards the victims were conspicuously absent, and the incidents conformed more or less closely to the pattern of deluded altruism. Since several examples of the kind were given in the last chapter, further instances need not be quoted here, but attention may be directed instead to the important minority of cases in which the motives appeared more aggressive.

(2) *Hostile Motives in Melancholics*

One of the first authorities to raise doubts whether the motives for violence in depressive illness should be accepted uncritically on superficial appearances was none other than Sigmund Freud. While few of the present day psycho-analysts support the 'death-instinct' theory, which Freud put forward in this connection, most of them accept the existence of an innate aggressive drive, although this is generally seen as an urge to dominate others rather than an urge to self-destruction.[1] But, however questionable his theoretical super-structure, Freud made some penetrating observations on the behaviour and ways of thought of depressed patients. In his classic essay *Mourning and Melancholia* (1917), he compared the symptoms of melancholia to the normal reaction of grief following loss of a loved one. In both conditions the despondent individual takes no interest in the outside world, lacks energy and zest, and feels that life has lost its purpose. In the normal grief reaction this is

[1] O. Fenichel, *The Psycho-analytic Theory of Neurosis*, 1945

explained as a forced turning away of libidinal energy from the outside world, and a temporary preoccupation with private fantasies and memories of the loved one who has gone. Might not pathological depression consist of a special instance of this kind, a loss of love object followed by a similar but more intense experience of inward directed libido? This would leave unexplained the special features of melancholia, the self-reproach, the delusions of extreme sinfulness, worthlessness and the craving for punishment, none of which occur in ordinary grief. At this point Freud made his most original suggestion. If the libidinal attachment had been both intense and ambivalent, a mixture of love and hate, the fantasied incorporation of the lost object into the self, and the turning inwards of libido, would release upon the self all the destructive aggressive energy that had hitherto been bound up with some external object. Introjection of the object of hatred would explain why such patients should accuse themselves of the very same things for which they once reviled someone else, and why they should try to punish themselves and even destroy themselves. Freud wrote:

'It is true we have long known that no neurotic harbours thoughts of suicide which are not murderous impulses against others redirected upon himself, but we have never been able to explain what interplay for forces could carry such a purpose through to execution. Now the analysis of melancholia shows that the ego can kill itself only when, the object-cathexis having been withdrawn upon it, it can treat itself as an object, when it is able to launch against itself the animosity relating to an object . . .'[1]

In spite of the Alice-in-Wonderland quality of this interpretation, there is much to be said for it. In common experience, even normal mood swings are associated with aggression. One says of a gloomy-looking person 'I wouldn't like to cross him', and everyone knows the combination of misery and annoyance called 'sulks'. Freud himself noted that melancholics 'are far from evincing towards those around them the attitude of humility and submission that alone would befit such worthless persons.' In fact, the admixture of aggressiveness which may

[1] *Mourning and Melancholia* (1917), p. 162

have brought about the failure of their personal relationships, also shows in their readiness to take offence even when depressed. No one who has had to deal with such patients in hospital would doubt that many of them give an impression of smouldering resentment and annoyance, mostly self-directed, but ever liable to spill over on to relatives and doctors.

Although the theory that ingrowing hate provides the basic psychopathology of depressive illness has aroused wide interest, not much has been published by way of systematic validation of these impressions. Some confirmatory evidence has emerged from studies of the early background of persons who have committed suicide. It appears that many suicidal persons have had adverse childhood experiences, in the form of loss of or rejection by parents, of the same general type as have been held responsible for the development of aggressive and psychopathic personality traits. Conversely, it appears that aggressive psychopaths are specially prone to both depressive moods and suicidal tendency. H. J. Walton carried out a systematic comparison of the suicidal and non-suicidal groups in a sample of depressed patients in hospital.[1] (Incidentally only a minority of the patients appeared suicidal or admitted to suicidal intentions on questioning.) None of the features commonly referred to in this connection, such as age, adverse living conditions, social isolation or severity of symptoms, in fact distinguished the suicidal group. The only factor found significantly more often in the suicidal cases was a history of early deprivation of parental affection, as indicated by loss of a parent or gross disharmony between parents. This finding supports the suggestion that the more openly aggressive among depressed patients, who are naturally the ones to come predominantly from backgrounds known to foster aggression, are also the ones most liable to turn their violence against themselves and die by suicide.

Further evidence of the aggressiveness of melancholics comes from an examination of their psychotic thought processes. One cannot usually demonstrate in the individual case the precise psychological mechanisms described by Freud, for even where these exist they are largely unconscious and have to be deduced from the patient's less guarded words and actions.

[1] 'Suicidal Behaviour in Depressive Illness,' *Journ. Mental Science*, 1958

Nevertheless, an underlying hostility towards the persons who should command their strongest affection, is sometimes quite apparent, even to clinicians with no particular leanings towards Freudian theory. Long ago Norwood East[1] pointed out that 'although it is probably correct to regard the typical melancholic homicide as altruistic in intention, cases occur in which the murder is traceable to less worthy motives'. He proceeded to quote the example of a depressed man who had delusions about his wife's infidelity, and heard 'voices' telling of her misdeeds, as a result of which he took a razor and slit her throat and then his own. Now delusions of jealousy, like delusions of being deceived, cheated, spied upon, sexually molested, or bewitched and magically tortured, are classed as persecutory, and are characteristically symptoms of paranoid schizophrenia rather than of depressive psychosis. Furthermore, paranoid patients do not ordinarily show any marked feelings of depression, or try to kill themselves, instead they give voice to undisguised hostility to others in the form of threats of retaliation against the injustice of their imaginary persecutors, though fortunately they do not often carry out their threats.

When psychotic patients commit acts of violence, the melancholic most typically destroys himself, while the paranoid schizophrenic, under the influence of delusory grievances, attacks the persons he thinks responsible for his wrongs; but states of mind intermediate between these two are commoner than generally realized. Dr P. G. McGrath, Medical Superintendent of Broadmoor Hospital, in reviewing some examples of homicide by depressives,[2] noted that altruistic motives are too readily accepted in such cases. Some indeed do conform to the classic formulation, as for instance when a devoted husband kills his wife under the delusions that they face ruin and had better die together. Others, however, even though definitely depressive, and even though they have made a serious suicidal attempt following homicide, when followed up in Broadmoor reveal unsuspected ideas of grievance, usually connected with marital disputes and infidelities, which must have been present when they attacked their victim. Some depressive murderers

---

[1] *Introduction to Forensic Psychiatry* (London, 1927), p. 332

[2] 'Personal Communication' (based on a talk at the Quarterly Meeting of the Royal Medico-Psychological Association, May 1963)

subsequently develop definite symptoms of schizophrenia, such as blunting of emotion and bizarre delusions, which cast doubt upon the original diagnosis.

A good example of a depressive murderer with delusions of distinctly paranoid flavour is quoted by J. H. Morton.[1] This was a married woman who drowned her child of 9, and attempted to drown herself at the same time. She had been under treatment from her family doctor, who noticed that she had started to worry unduly about small matters and had referred to having done a great wrong, which turned out to be a trivial technical offence. Before the drowning, she scribbled a note to her husband: 'I am sorry it has come to this, but we are better off it is all through your mother also Mrs – . . . there are too many spies . . .' Under observation she was depressed, and unable to occupy herself, and at the same time morbidly suspicious and convinced that some fellow-patients were spies. The symptoms lasted a few months, after which she became bright and cheerful and able to work. A second example quoted by Morton, while still in between classical schizophrenia and depression, showed more definite schizophrenic features. This was a widow who murdered her child of 11. She said that white slave traders were going to take her girl away, and rather than let that happen she should kill her. She had written crazy letters to the vicar proposing marriage and warning of the dangers of the white slave traffic. She was also deluded that she had caught cancer from her husband, who had died of the disease, and that she might give it to others and that she ought to kill herself with carbolic acid. She did not do so, although the bottle was found in her house. In Broadmoor she quietened down, but her paranoid delusions persisted.

The American psychiatrist, J. D. Campbell has challenged the 'altruistic' interpretation of depressive murder even in cases without schizophrenic features.[2] He points out that the emotional and physiological disturbances in depression may bring about episodes of destructive *furor* during which ideas of jealousy and retaliation may be acted upon impulsively. Those to whom the patient is most intimately attached are selected

[1] op. cit.

[2] *Manic-Depressive Disease* (Philadelphia and London, 1953), p. 295

as victims because they are the ones who can most readily arouse his morbid sensitiveness, since, as Freud pointed out, it is the people we have loved that we are also able to hate most intensively. In illustration of this Campbell quoted the example of a depressed woman, dull and retarded on examination, with numerous hypochondriacal complaints and fears of syphilis, cancer, etc., who shot her husband dead and then swallowed fly killer in an attempt to commit suicide. She manifested periodic temper tantrums in which she complained that everyone was watching her and expecting her to die, and it was in the course of just such an outburst that she had killed her husband. Campbell also cited the example of a typically guilt-ridden melancholic, obsessed with sin and religious anxieties, who destroyed his entire family because, he said, his wife was too flippant and light-hearted in her attitude to life and the children were too innocent to be reared in this sinful world. The mixture of aggressive and condemnatory ideas with thoughts of mercy-killing was well shown by the man's further comment that his wife would anyway not have been happy to go on living without her children.

In the present survey, among the insane offenders of the main murder-suicide sample the influence of hostile, paranoid delusions was more apparent in the schizophrenics than in the depressives, but as has been pointed out some of these were suffering from psychoses of mixed symptomatology, and classification as either depressives or schizophrenics was rather arbitrary. Among those considered depressives, paranoid thinking was occasionally evident, as for instance in Case 77 (p. 68), the depressed woman with delusions about her husband's fidelity who became wildly jealous and aggressive to the point of murder. Paranoid delusions of this kind are so obviously dangerous in content that there is some tendency to forget that other types of delusion, such as the hypochondriacal ideas mentioned above, can also become so through the involvement of persons with whom the patient feels strong identification. A good example of this was the following:

Case 63
A man of fifty, very conscientious about his work, a keen member of his church, and described as a quiet, retiring, uncommunicative

person, had shown signs of depressive illness for a whole year before his death. The first signs were worrying and loss of confidence following a promotion to more responsible work. He gave this up nine months before his death, and felt better for a time, but developed self-reproachful feelings about having let down his family.

Two months before his death he was seen by a psychiatrist who found him tense and self-reproachful, saying that he had wrecked his wife's and daughter's lives. He was advised to go into hospital, but he declined. He returned home and became progressively more disturbed, until he was finally pacing up and down making agitated allusions to his wickedness and his fears that he would become a raving lunatic and that he had driven his wife and daughter mad too. Seriously alarmed by his behaviour, his relatives contacted a doctor, but before arrangements had been made for his admission he had killed his wife and daughter and himself and left behind a suicide note expressing his delusions of unforgivable sin and his desire to save his family from a similar fate.

The above example also illustrates a further important aspect of some of these dangerous depressive cases, namely their unwillingness to follow medical advice and the questionable policy of many medical authorities who will invoke compulsory powers only in extreme cases.

In discussing motives for psychotic violence one tends perhaps to over-emphasize the content of the delusory thinking and to pay insufficient attention to the sheer pressure of extreme emotional tension which may result in desperate violence. Many authorities have been struck by the calm which sometimes follows a murderous outburst, as in the following case reported by Rabin:[1]

The murderer was happily married, but described as shy and seclusive, and thought to suffer from an inferiority complex. At the age of 38 he developed a depressive illness in which he became actively suicidal, the illness was probably familial, for his father had hanged himself many years previously. During this illness he expressed paranoid fears that the state authorities were after him on account of some form he had once filled in wrongly. He was admitted to hospital and treated by electroplexy and showed some

---

[1] 'Homicide and Attempted Suicide,' *Amer. Journ. Orthopsychiatry*, 1946

improvement. Unfortunately, his relatives insisted on taking him away too soon, and shortly after his return he once again became very agitated by the same persecutory fears. During a woodland walk, on which he was accompanied by his wife, he struck her dead with a chopper, also killed the dogs that were with them, and then slit his own throat and wrists very severely indeed. He was rescued and taken back to hospital, where he was able to explain that he had killed his wife and his dogs because he had been convinced he was hopelessly insane and he did not wish them to suffer through his removal to hospital. The Rorschach personality test, which had been applied during his previous stay in hospital, was repeated. The results confirmed the clinical impression that he had improved, and was emotionally less constricted and tense.

Rabin considered that this case showed that the 'extended suicide' type of crime has much in common with psychotic murders that are not necessarily associated with suicide. In this case, as in the examples of murderous psychotic outbursts described by Wertham[1] under the heading of 'catathymic crisis', the offender perceives the violent act as a solution to an intolerable state of tension. After commission of the crime tension is lowered and a phase of superficial normality follows.

The partial return of sanity following a desperate act can have most unfortunate consequences for the offender. Woddis[2] cites the case of a man of 30 who stabbed his wife to death. Relatives had noticed a change in him during the year previous. Although normally very active, he had stopped working, neglected his appearance, and sat for long periods not speaking, sighing and rubbing his hands. He had been brooding over suicide for a long time and had tried to obtain a gun with which to shoot his wife and children and himself. Finally he stabbed his wife impulsively with a kitchen knife during a quarrel. Subsequently he displayed no further symptoms and was hanged.

(3) *Danger Signals in Depressive Illness*
In spite of it being very well known that psychotic depressives may attack others as well as themselves, surprisingly few investigators have concerned themselves with determining the

[1] *The Show of Violence* (New York and London, 1949)
[2] 'Depression and Crime,' *Brit. Journ. Delinquency*, 1957

extent of the risk or how it may vary from one case to the next. Some direct evidence of the extent of murderous aggression among depressed patients comes from an investigation by J. C. Batt who found that once a clinician's interest is aroused sufficiently to put direct questions on the matter it becomes apparent that many such patients have experienced homicidal thoughts which they have been naturally reluctant to express spontaneously. These homicidal fantasies are by no means restricted to the 'altruistic' thought that the victim would be better off dead.[1]

Confirmation of the existence of this close link between aggressive tendencies and depressive illness does not mean that the risk of any given patient committing murder is very great. Fortunately very few patients act upon their murderous thoughts. Over 20,000 patients are admitted annually to the mental hospitals in England and Wales for the treatment of depressive psychosis, and of course there are others who remain at home. In any particular year it must be something of the order of one in a thousand of those suffering from depressive psychosis who commit murder.

In his research, Batt tried to find out what clinical features distinguished the small minority of patients who translated their homicidal thoughts into action. He collected a series of twenty patients who had committed some homicidal attack in the course of a depressive illness. Nineteen of them were women who had attacked their children. The method of selection may have exaggerated this trend since murderous assaults by men, or assaults on adults, are more likely to lead to admission to a Special Hospital than are attacks by mothers on their children, which may be dealt with by admitting the offender to the ordinary mental hospitals from which Batt drew his cases. However, granting that women with small children, if they go into a depression, present a particular risk of homicide, this is more likely due to the defencelessness of their potential victims than to any excess of aggression among female compared with male depressives.

Another point of interest noted by Batt was that the age of his homicidal depressed women (average $29\frac{1}{2}$ years, with 60%

[1] 'Homicidal Incidence in the Depressive Psychoses,' *Journ. Mental Science,* 1948

in the range 25 up to 35 years) was significantly younger than expected for patients admitted to hospital with depressive psychosis. He suggested that this youthfulness could be due to the fact that homicidal acts occur usually in a first attack, when relatives are unprepared for what the illness involves, and the patient is left too long without care and supervision. The youthfulness of Batt's homicidal depressives might also be explained as a consequence of the fact that only relatively young women as a rule have the care of small children. According to Batt's interpretation the low average age of depressed murderers should hold true for both sexes, but the present findings do not support this. There was a distinct preponderance of women among the depressive offenders of the main murder-suicide sample (in the ratio of 21 women to 7 men), and the women were relatively young. A half of them fell in the age decade 25 to 35, which was very similar to Batt's finding. In the case of male offenders, however, the depressive cases were a distinctly older group.

Table 16 sets out the age distribution of the depressive offenders in the main murder-suicide sample against the age distribution of patients admitted to hospitals in England and Wales in the year 1959 with the diagnosis of manic-depressive psychosis, as given in the Registrar-General's Statistical Review. Even compared with patients admitted for the first time, the murderous females are unusually young, whereas the male offenders, so far as can be judged from such a very small number, are just as old as any ordinary group of depressives in hospital. Since the victims of depressed women were nearly always their own small children it is probably the special liability of being a young mother of a small child, rather than just being a young person experiencing a first attack of depression, which makes for homicidal risk.

Returning to Batt's survey, he remarked upon another important feature. With one doubtful exception, all of his cases, even if they had not made an actual suicidal attempt, were considered to have been in an actively suicidal phase of their illness at the time they made their homicidal assaults. Since only a minority of depressives are actively suicidal,[1] this observation furnishes a quite important lead to the identification of

[1] H. J. Walton, op. cit.

dangerous cases. Incidentally, it also provides support for the theory that both the homicidal and the suicidal tendencies among these patients have a common root in pathological aggression.

A little reflection upon some of the factors long known to be associated with suicide among depressives does suggest some plausible reasons why homicidal and suicidal risks should be present together in the same group of patients. For instance, a particular risk of suicide exists during phases of development and recovery, when the symptoms are less severe, and those in charge of the patient are less vigilant. At the very height of a paralysing attack, if the patient is confused and severely retarded, perhaps even speechless and stuporous, he is in no state to take effective and resolute action, either against himself or others, and in any event when symptoms have reached such a pitch the patient finds himself under close supervision in hospital. When depressed patients commit suicide after discharge from hospital the time most frequently chosen is quite soon after leaving, presumably before they have fully recovered.[1]

This fact has long been known to clinical observers such as E. Kraepelin[2] who wrote: 'just in convalescence the danger of suicide is often especially great . . . Many patients also wish to leave the institution only on that account, in order to be able to accomplish their suicidal intentions outside. In such cases they often manage to conceal their real mood with great skill . . .' Similarly, in the phase of partial development of the illness, especially in first attacks when relatives do not know what to watch for, patients may for a long time succeed in concealing their inner torment from those around them. For instance, a depressed woman student, suffering a first attack, appeared outwardly normal, except for unexplained lethargy and inefficiency. Under the delusion that she was hopelessly unworthy of her parents efforts on her behalf, she secretly plotted to kill herself, but took care to pretend to be interested in plans being made for her. She prepared for a day when she would be left alone and undisturbed in the house, and when that

[1] A. Capstick, op. cit.

[2] *Manic-Depressive Insanity and Paranoia*, translated by R. M. Barclay (Edinburgh, 1921)

happened she first waited till the expected delivery men had called, then carefully drew the curtain and turned on the gas. Only by the merest fluke of chance was she discovered, revived, and her unspoken delusions subsequently elicited. It would be of interest to find out how many of the murder-suicide crimes are committed by depressed patients recently discharged from hospital, or by persons not yet diagnosed as depressives who nevertheless show incipient symptoms of the disorder. Probably the most important factor of all in connection with homicidal risk is the ability of some patients to keep their outward symptoms unobtrusive over a long period until, as Batt put it, the true mental condition is discovered by the police, after tragedy has occurred, instead of beforehand by the doctor.

The findings of the present survey were in line with the anticipation that murder-suicides in the course of depressive illness would tend to occur at periods when suicidal risk is at its greatest, particularly during the evolutionary phase of depressive psychosis, often in the first few weeks of a first attack, rather than when the sufferer is widely incapacitated or when the diagnosis and its implications are known to the relatives. So far as could be ascertained, out of the 28 depressives counted as 'insane', 8 had been ill for less than a month, and not more than 7 had had a depressive illness previously. In 14 cases, the warning symptoms were not particularly obvious, and certainly not such as to lead to any expectation of tragedy. On the other hand, in a minority of cases, about 8 in number, recent attempts or threats of violence against the self or others, or the obvious gravity of the mental disturbance, might have justified compulsory admission to hospital. The following example, which presents a complete contrast to Case 77 quoted on page 68, illustrates the wide range of variation in this respect, and shows how serious symptoms may sometimes be quite unobtrusive and their significance easily missed:

Case 35
One morning, after seeing her husband off to work as usual, a young wife killed her infant son and herself by stuffing rugs and papers against the doors and turning on the gas. Husband, relatives and neighbours were all taken completely by surprise as she had seemed cheerful, fit and free from worry and had not

been previously subject to depression, although she was regarded as a very quiet, reserved person.

A few weeks before her death she had told her husband and her mother that she had a pain in her chest, and referred to her father's death from cancer a few years previously. They urged her to go to her doctor for an examination, which she did, but although she mentioned a cough she did not tell her doctor of her fear of cancer. As she appeared well and cheerful after seeing the doctor, her family assumed she had been reassured. There were no significant financial or marital problems, and the only plausible conclusion appears to be that the unfortunate woman was overwhelmed by a secret fear or delusion that she had a malignant disease.

A further point about homicidal risk, one not mentioned by Batt, concerns the influence of long-standing personality traits upon the form of the psychotic symptoms. Evidence has been accumulating from comparative studies showing that cultural trends, for example the Italian tendency to open expression of physical aggression, may show themselves in the kind of symptoms displayed during psychotic illness, in this example by an excess of aggressive behaviour among the patients of Italian origin.[1] It is regrettably well known to psychiatrists who have to deal with them that aggressive criminals and anti-social types do not lose their unpleasant attributes if they happen to develop a psychotic illness; in fact if anything they may become worse, plaguing other patients with their spitefulness or temper, and plaguing the staff with their unco-operativeness and tendency to abscond. For these reasons one suspects that a history of aggressiveness of personality previous to the onset of depressive illness may foreshadow an increase in homicidal risk during the psychotic phase. This question is closely tied to what is an important issue for doctors in charge of depressed patients, namely whether those who have once been homicidal while depressed are especially liable to become so again if they suffer a relapse.

Scrutiny of the psychiatric literature gives little help on this

---

[1] M. Opler *et al.*, 'Ethnic differences in Behaviour and Psychopathology,' *Internat. Journ. Soc. Psychiatry*, 1956; B. Fantl and J. Schiro, 'Cultural Variables in the Behaviour of Schizophrenics', *Internat. Journ. Soc. Psychiatry*, 1959

point although isolated case reports do suggest that murderous impulses are apt to recur. Woddis, when quoting some typical examples of serious crimes committed under the influence of depressive illness, mentions an unusual case of a man who actually presented himself at an out-patient clinic with the complaint that he feared he might kill somebody, perhaps his wife.[1] He had once before, when depressed, shot a fellow serviceman, and served a sentence of detention for the crime. On examination he was found to be morbidly depressed and retarded, but recovered satisfactorily with treatment, and lost his fear of committing murder.

The present survey was on too small a scale for any firm answer to emerge, but it is at least suggestive that in several instances among the group of depressive offenders there was a history of previous attempts or threats of violence. Such was the case in the following example, which also illustrates in addition the well-known point that the period immediately following discharge from hospital is one of special risk:

Case 9
An elderly man who had pursued a very respectable, industrious life and enjoyed a long and happy marriage was sent to hospital by his doctor for 'bizarre symptoms of depression'. He complained that life was empty and he wanted the end to come, and he had attempted to electrocute himself. He had made threats and one desultory attempt to take his wife's life because she was ill and he felt the situation hopeless. After three weeks in hospital he was judged 'considerably improved from his acute depressed phase' and was allowed to take his discharge. Ten days later he killed his wife with a chopper, wrote a brief despairing note to his son, and then gassed himself.

Another point about the risk of violence in psychotic depressives concerns the symptoms of anguished restlessness, frequently coupled with hypochondrical delusions, which, in the sub-group of illness called agitated depression, largely displaces the customary listlessness and retardation. These agitated patients are known to clinicians to present greater risk of suicide. J. D. Campbell points out that whereas patients with severe depression, entirely bereft of hope, may not

[1] op. cit.

attempt suicide, others who are particularly distressed about some single physical symptom, such as insomnia, will kill themselves.[1] He confirms Henderson and Gillespie's statement that: 'We have known cases, almost monosymptomatic in character – perhaps only a persistent headache, without physical signs, but with a good deal of concern about it – who committed suicide.'[2] That these agitated, hypochondriacal patients may also carry a greater homicidal risk is suggested by Sullivan who wrote:

> . . . and it may be noted that this [hypochondrical element] is relatively frequent in melancholic murder, and may possibly suggest that the delusional emphasis in these cases on the visceral condition indicates a greater degree of disorder of organic function from which the homicidal impulse would be more apt to develop.[3]

Agitation and hypochondriasis were prominent symptoms in a number of the depressed murder-suicide offenders in the present survey, thus confirming the need to take such symptoms very seriously when they occur in the course of a depressive illness. Several examples illustrating the effect of hypochondriacal fears have been quoted (e.g. Cases 9, 27, 33 and 35), including the classic instance of the man who murdered his family under the delusion that he had infected them all with venereal disease. Many other instances were equally striking in the prominence of hypochondriacal delusions. One middle-aged mother of an only child (Case 53) became convinced she was pregnant and fretted continually about this in spite of repeated reassurances to the contrary from her doctor. She left a suicide note explaining that she could not survive having another child and the hospital would do nothing to help. She had better gas her child as well to save her husband being left to look after it. Another middle-aged woman who gassed her small daughter and herself (Case 62) had been complaining of pains in her head and neck, and began to neglect her house cleaning. She left behind a note confessing her fear that she was going out of her mind. In another very similar case (Case 34) a mother who had had a history of previous depressions developed a groundless

[1] op. cit., p. 305
[2] *Textbook of Psychiatry* (Oxford, 1947)
[3] op. cit., p. 93

fear of cancer, which her husband did not take seriously until she had gassed her child and herself. Another mother (Case 52) with a 2-month-old baby complained that her head was in a whirl and left behind a suicide note explaining that she knew there was something wrong in her mind and that the children were being affected.

While some individuals, notably among the elderly, manifest agitation, restlessness and hypochondrical fears more severely than others, all psychotic depressives tend to have such symptoms during certain phases of their illness. Kraines has described six phases, 1 and 2 being phases of onset and development; 3 and 4 being phases of deep melancholia, with complete retardation, inability to talk or to work, and nihilistic delusions; 5 and 6 being phases of recovery.[1] During both the initial and terminal phases mood is subject to greater fluctuation, and anxieties, fears and hypochondrical complaints are voiced more insistently than during the deepest phases of depression. Irritability occurs with special severity in phases 2 and 5, when the patients are too ill to work off their feelings by concentrating feverishly upon tasks in hand. Then everything seems an irritant, they can't bear to listen to stupid conversation or blaring radio, they fear they are 'going to pieces', they react violently to the slightest criticism, and snap at friends and relatives for the most trivial reason. Sometimes violent hostility develops, based upon resentments which previously were dealt with reasonably, but now appear so unbearable as to produce outbursts of murderous feelings. 'This desire to strike out, to destroy, is the extreme expression of irritability and so is usually present in phases 2 and 5 when irritability is most intense. Rarely does it occur in the complete apathy of phases 3 and 4.'[2] Kraines himself regarded these mental phases as concomitants of neurological states of varying excitability, but regardless of their cause the fact that they tend to occur on either side of the main trough of depression provides an additional indication of the danger spots of the depressive cycle.

An important question, and one rarely discussed, is to what extent homicidal tendency, which is well recognized in connection with depressive psychosis, also occurs in that very

[1] *Mental Depressions and their Treatment* (New York, 1957)
[2] ibid., p. 245

common form of depressive illness where the symptoms fall short of outright madness and the condition is classed as neurotic. The characteristics of psychotic depression, the hereditary predisposition, the periodicity of the illness (which is tied to age, but appears to have only slight relation to external circumstances), the seriousness of the symptoms (which can well lead to starvation and death quite apart from violent suicide), and the favourable response to physical methods of treatment, suggest some basic constitutional fault, probably of a biochemical nature, and favour the theory that melancholia is really an endogenous physical disease which produces mental symptoms much as a high fever produces delirium. In general clinical experience, however, one more frequently encounters, especially among individuals of neurotic temperament, instances of depressive reactions which appear to have been precipitated by some misfortune or personal difficulty. Such responses can rightly be called illnesses, since in intensity and duration they are out of all proportion to what might be considered a 'normal' reaction to the provoking circumstances, but they do not usually progress as far as mental confusion and delusions.

In the past, considerable controversy has centred on the status of these two forms of depression, some authorities, such as Aubrey Lewis, suggesting that they represent different degrees of severity, others maintaining that they are distinct entities. The position has been reviewed by Kiloh and Garside.[1] It seems that recent evidence (including the observations that endogenous psychotic depressives respond better to modern physical treatments, have lower thresholds to the effects of sedative drugs, have less neurotic and psychopathic traits in the intervals between attacks, and show more indications of physical disturbance such as weight loss and diurnal variation in symptoms), all tends to favour the view that endogenous and neurotic depression are distinct entities.

In Walton's study of suicides among depressed patients in hospital,[2] he grouped the patients into neurotic reactive and endogenous psychotic cases. The incidence of suicide was

[1] 'The Independence of Neurotic Depression and Endogenous Depression,' *Brit. Journ. Psychiatry*, 1963
[2] op. cit.

equally high in both groups. This rather surprising conclusion suggests that perhaps outwardly directed violence also may occur among neurotic depressives. The fact that so many murder-suicide incidents take place outside hospital, presumably committed by depressed persons who are not under restraint because they do not appear mad, further suggests that some of these crimes occur in states of neurotic rather than psychotic illness.

On the theory that the extreme disturbance of behaviour represented by murderous violence would occur only in a state of florid psychosis of endogenous origin, in which the patient is obviously overwhelmed by mental confusion and delusions, one would expect a history of previous attacks of depression, either in the patient himself or in other members of the family, to be readily elicited in most cases. Such expectations were actually fulfilled in one very small sample of 9 murderous depressive patients studied in Italy.[1] All of these were apparently in an advanced state of melancholia when they committed their crimes, all of them had had at least two previous episodes of depressive psychosis, and all but two had other members of the family with a history of suicide, psychosis or dysthymia.

The present findings were quite different. In the first place, as is the case with suicide, many of the offenders in the murder-suicide sample were neurotic reactive depressives rather than examples of typical endogenous illness. Even though, for the sake of clarity in analysis, only those offenders reported to have shown definite signs of mental illness were included in the group labelled 'depressives', a considerable proportion were of the neurotic reactive type, and less than a quarter were reported as having had any similar attack previously. Furthermore, some of those described as 'relatively normal' offenders were undoubtedly experiencing depressive reactions of varying degrees of severity. As far as the present survey is concerned, therefore, neurotic reactive depression would seem to rank equally with psychotic depression as a factor of importance in murder-suicide.

Finally, one feature said to distinguish murder by depressives from other kinds of murder is the time of day chosen for the act.

[1] C. Citterio et al., 'Psicosi depressive e criminalità', Il Lavoro Neuropsichiatrico, 1962

Gibbens, on the basis of his comparison between sane and insane homicides in New Jersey, concluded that depressed murderers . . . 'have a noticeable tendency to murder between 6.0 a.m. and 8.0 a.m.'[1] Such a finding would fit in rather nicely with the clinical observation that endogenous depressives are prone to early waking with an accompanying exacerbation of symptoms at that time.

In the present sample, so many murderers and their victims died quietly of gas poisoning, leaving their bodies to be discovered many hours later, that in many cases the precise time of the homicidal act could not be established. In a few cases suicide notes written at the time gave more or less exact information. Thus, in Case 72, the murderer, who wrote his last words while he was himself feeling the effects of poisoning, indicated that he had turned on the gas to annihilate his family at 2.0 a.m. Sometimes the temperature of the bodies, or the moment when a victim was last seen by a neighbour, helped to establish the time of the murder within a reasonable span. In a few cases the time was fixed by the overheard commotion of shooting or violence. In Case 33, the murderer called out that they were 'only larking' when a neighbour overheard his victim's screams.

Within the limitations set by uncertain information, some attempt was made to fix the probable times of murders in the main sample, and to contrast the times chosen by those diagnosed as suffering from depressive illness with the times chosen by the remainder of the offenders. Table 17 shows the results. Most murders, whether depressive or otherwise, occurred in the middle of the day or late at night. Nevertheless, when an early morning killing did occur, it was more often associated with a depressive offender, but the effect was too slight for statistical significance with such small numbers.

[1] op. cit.

IX

The Psychology of Murder-Suicide by Sane Persons

(1) *Murder and Suicide as Alternative forms of Aggression*

ACCORDING to instinct theory, destructive behaviour satisfies a basic, inborn aggressive drive which, like hunger or sex, requires periodic satisfaction through appropriate tension-relieving activity. Aggression must find some outlet, either in violence to the self or to others, or in a combination of both, and which form is taken will depend upon external circumstances.

Clinical studies have generally been held to favour this instinct theory of aggression. Increases in aggressiveness produced by changes in internal hormone levels, or by neurological injuries, fit in with the picture of an internal source of aggressive energy which must find an outlet somehow or other. Psychoanalysts have contributed significantly to this way of thinking, and none more than Freud himself, who, in his later writings, having been deeply impressed by the destructive elements seen in wars and sadistic cruelties, postulated a 'death instinct' at the root of human aggression. Opposed to the life instincts (*Eros*), that find release of tension through gregarious, co-operative and sexual behaviour, Freud imagined the death instinct (*Thanatos*) seeking release in the calm of ultimate extinction. That life manages to continue notwithstanding Freud explained as follows: 'A more fruitful idea was that a portion of the death instinct is diverted towards the external world and comes to light as an instinct of aggressiveness. In this way the instinct itself could be pressed into the service of *Eros*, in that the organism was destroying some other thing, whether animate or inanimate, instead of destroying its own self.'[1] In other words, man spares himself by attacking others.

[1] Freud, S. *Civilisation and its Discontents*, 1930

113

In the passage just quoted Freud immediately goes on to state: 'Conversely, any restriction of this aggressiveness directed outwards would be bound to increase the self-destruction . . .' In common with other modern exponents of the same theory, Banen applies the idea to homicide and suicide and concludes: 'Just as love and hate, passivity and aggressiveness, and sadism and masochism are, so to speak, opposite sides of the same coin, so are suicide and homicide and all its variants; the difference being that in the former the aggression is internalized, whereas in the latter it is externalized.'[1]

It is not only the insane who may find self-destruction a substitute for attacks against others. The mental gymnastics described by Freud in explanation of the behaviour of melancholics could apply to suicides in general. Most students of the subject, regardless of whether they support the particular interpretations advanced by Freud, have been impressed by the aggressive features in many suicides, especially those committed in the heat of rage or jealousy.

An intensive clinical study of cases of suicide and serious suicidal attempts was carried out by the psycho-analyst Karl Menninger who claimed to have discovered many examples conforming to the pattern of Freudian theory.[2] In place of the popularly accepted notion of self-effacement and sad surrender before a harsh fate, Menninger more often found a fierce aggressive urge ready to vent itself in self-punishment and self-destruction if no other outlet presented. As an example, he quoted the case of an investor, ruined by failures on the stock-market, who killed himself, but not before he had prepared a written explanation of his action which laid blame on his brokers. In another instance quoted, a man similarly affected by stock-market failure actually murdered his broker before killing himself. This illustration shows the surprisingly close resemblance psychologically between many ordinary suicides and the murder-suicide cases with which this report is concerned.

Sometimes the aggressive urge is divided so evenly between homicidal and suicidal impulses that some quite trifling circumstance may have sufficient weight to tip the scales one way or the other. A. L. Wood, in the course of a description of

---

[1] 'Suicide by Psychotics,' *Jour. Nervous and Mental Disease*, 1954
[2] *Man Against Himself* (New York, 1938)

the sort of homicide and suicide incidents prevalent in Ceylon, quoted the case of a 24-year-old man who constantly quarrelled with the mistress with whom he was living. She was a married woman whose husband was in prison. A violent quarrel began one morning when he objected that the dress she was wearing to go out on an errand was immodest. She refused to change and they came to blows. He drew a knife and threatened to stab her. She fell on her knees and begged him not to kill her whereupon he said, 'All right! I won't stab you! I will stab myself!' He did so and died.[1]

The hair's breadth division between murder and suicide in many a rejected lover is well illustrated by a case quoted by Neustatter.[2] The example also shows the strange mixture of self-blame and aggression which is the hall-mark of such tragedies. A hitherto well-behaved, gentle young man was told by his fiancée that she wanted to break their engagement. He was very upset and cried, and she agreed to go for a walk with him to talk things over. He took a knife with him with the intention of killing himself if she did not relent. Once before, when posted to a lonely spot by the army, he had become depressed and attempted suicide. During their walk (according to the offender at the moment he was about to give the girl a farewell kiss) he impulsively strangled her. He admitted no conscious awareness of anger. On subsequent examination he was depressed and so slow and apathetic in manner as to be taken for a defective, although his intelligence was average. Later he became inappropriately placid, commenting on the kindness of people towards him, and saying he was feeling better. (Such a hysterical denial of unbearable remorse is not uncommon in mental patients who have committed dreadful crimes, and probably occurs during recovery from their acute disturbance, when the full reality of their situation begins to dawn upon them.)

Psycho-analytic studies of actual murderers, especially of those who have committed impulsive and to outward appearances somewhat irrational crimes, have confirmed the equivalence in unconscious fantasy of suicidal and homicidal ideas

[1] 'Crime and Aggression in Ceylon,' *Trans. Am. Phil. Soc.*, 1961, p. 64
[2] 'Psychiatric Aspects of Diminished Responsibility in Murder,' *Medico-Legal Jour.*, 1960, p. 95

as well as their inter-changeability in action. Hyatt Williams, in a clinical survey of a number of men who had murdered women and were afterwards treated on psycho-analytic lines in an English prison,[1] found suicidal tendencies very prevalent in these offenders. Their crimes were the results of 'projective identification', a process whereby internal, unconscious fantasies of a highly aggressive nature were projected into a scapegoat. Through their victims' deaths, these murderers destroyed a part of themselves, but they were just as likely to try to effect the same kind of destruction by means of attempted suicide. In one example quoted by Hyatt Williams (Case 3) a young man killed his wife by giving her a lethal dose of poison when she pestered him for something with which to procure an abortion. He said he had originally bought the poison intending to take it himself, and in fact he had made a number of suicidal attempts. He was a fussy, meticulous person who was in open conflict with his wife because she was dirty and neglectful of their child. In the course of therapy, he became aware of a hitherto unconscious resentment against an over-possessive and dominating mother, and of a demonified image of a hateful, manipulating female which he was apt to project into any woman with whom he formed a close relationship. In addition, his wife's wish to destroy her baby had re-awakened his own childhood death wishes against any rival baby his mother might have produced, so that in destroying his wife he was also symbolically destroying his own wickedness. The probable correctness of these interpretations was indicated by the fact that realization and acceptance of these motives brought about a noticeable improvement in the prisoner's behaviour, which had previously been irritable, intolerant and generally immature, and was also accompanied by the disappearance of some troublesome skin complaints of psycho-somatic origin.

The type of suicide in which motives of spite or retaliation predominate recalls the custom, prevalent among some primitive peoples, of killing themselves at their enemy's door so as to expose him to the vengeance of their surviving relatives. Indeed, the threat 'it will be at your own door' shows a similar thought process in our own community. Menninger also cited

[1] 'The Psychopathology of sexual murderers,' in I. Rosen (Ed.), *The Pathology and Treatment of Sexual Deviation*, 1964

the occasional reports of boys hanging themselves after punishment, in which situation the motive of 'I'll show you, now you'll be sorry' seems particularly plain.

Ruth Cavan, in her extensive study of suicide, quoted examples of persons killing themselves after quarrels, and in circumstances which left no doubt that they were expressing anger. For instance, the young mistress of a married man, following a quarrel with her lover, wrote an aggrieved note to him beginning, 'I couldn't stand to let the mean things you do hurt and disappoint me any longer.'[1] In another example, a young businessman, jealous of his wife's social pretensions, killed himself after a long period of marital dissension, remarking in the course of a long suicide note: 'You have them now, your dear friends, and you can go out with them because you are free again.' Norwood East, in a survey of 1,000 consecutive cases of attempted suicide admitted to Brixton Prison, identified 'quarrels and temper' as a major factor in 12% of cases.[2] Stengel and others, in a more recent monograph, emphasize the manipulative value of attempted suicide, and show that in many cases the act performs the function of a desperate appeal, whereby the person hopes, perhaps unconsciously, to force somebody to deal with his problems.[3] In a study of 200 consecutive admissions to a general hospital in Edinburgh following attempted suicide I. R. C. Batchelor found that 21% (25 males and 17 females) were definitely psychopathic.[4] This large group, often neglected in discussions on suicide, showed the usual characteristics of psychopaths. Many were aggressive, and described as bullying, cantankerous, vindictive or jealous, and some were egotistical, cold and friendless. Social disturbance in the form of poverty, isolation, restlessness, frequent unemployment, alcoholism and sexual maladjustment was particularly marked. Of the 25 men, 5 were drug addicts, 5 chronic gamblers and 13 had police records. Of the total group, 74% came from broken homes and 71% were from the lowest social class. Their personality disturbance revealed itself unmistakably in the circumstances of their suicidal attempts,

[1] op. cit., p. 291
[2] 'On Attempted Suicide,' *Journ. Mental Science*, 1913
[3] op. cit.
[4] 'Psychopathic States and Attempted Suicide,' *Brit. Medical Journ.*, 1954

the majority of which were impulsive and precipitated by quarrels. Arrest or the threat of arrest was the second commonest stimulus. Hate was the most prominent motivation, aroused by quarrels with persons for whom they had had previously strong ambivalent feelings. 'In several cases it was quite obvious that the suicidal individual had felt strong provocation to murder.' In six instances serious attacks on other persons preceded the suicidal attempt. In over a quarter of cases motives of spite, pique or revenge were apparent, as in the example of the girl who, believing herself jilted, gassed herself while lying on her lover's bed. In a further analysis of the same series of cases Batchelor[1] identified 43 who gave a history of excessive drinking (including 19 who were also psychopaths). In most of these serious underlying personality disorder was evident, and the commonest antecedents were explosive quarrels, although among the cases who were alcoholic without being psychopathic the trend was less marked. Batchelor commented: 'Both alcoholism and attempted suicide are in themselves patently aggressive reactions. Causing so much offence to relatives and to society as a whole they give a sense of power.'

More recent studies of attempted suicides have confirmed the high incidence of personality disturbance. Kessel found marital disharmony to be the most outstanding factor.[2] Bruhn, comparing attempted suicide with patients attending a psychiatric out-patient department, found that the former had a more frequent history of broken home before the age of 15 (42% to 25%); more frequent unemployment (34% to 20%); more frequent change of address (38% to 22%) and very much more frequent marital disharmony (89% to 48%).[3]

In rare cases murder is committed by suicidal persons with the deliberate, self-conscious purpose of ending their own lives by judicial execution. Sellin, in a study of the effects of capital punishment, quoted a number of such cases.[4] One example, that of the murderer Robert Irwin, was reported in detail by

---

[1] 'Alcohol and Attempted Suicide,' *Journ. Mental Science*, 1954

[2] 'Attempted Suicide in Edinburgh,' *Scot. Medical Journ.*, 1962

[3] 'A comparative study of Attempted Suicides and Psychiatric Out-patients,' *Brit. Journ. Preventive Soc. Medicine*, 1963

[4] *The Death Penalty* (Philadelphia, 1951)

the doctor who had tried to treat him.[1] In the course of a psycho-analytic session, this man had described how he had at one time felt so sick and miserable that he would like to die. The aggressive thought then came to him that rather than commit suicide himself he would first kill his girl-friend (he was always feeling rejected by women) and then go to the electric chair for it. Not long after, again becoming depressed, the same idea recurred, only this time he acted upon it, killing not only a girl-friend, but also two of her associates. Afterwards he made enormously detailed confessions to the police. In other instances, similarly motivated killings have been more impersonal, the victim being some totally innocent stranger. Sometimes the wish to die by execution may be masked by a real or exaggerated desire for public attention, as in the famous case of Marjeram (cited by the Royal Commission on Capital Punishment), who killed a complete stranger on a common, apparently solely for the sake of the excitement and glamour of a public trial.

Psycho-analytic views on the deeper motives of suicide, especially as expounded by Menninger, can be roughly summarized under two headings. First comes the angry, aggressive component, a wish to kill or destroy. Second comes the process by which the aggression turns back upon the self. The initial, aggressive element is prominent in immature, psychopathic personalities, and also in those neurotic characters (whose disturbance may be better concealed from outside) whose attachments are ambivalent. Recoil of aggression into the self is apt to occur in individuals with a strong super-ego which prevents them from venting their rage externally, since awareness of their own murderous desires provokes intolerable guilt feelings and a need for punishment. Turning back of aggression is also apt to occur, as Zilborg pointed out,[2] following the interruption of an ambivalent attachment, for then the emotions no longer possess an external object. Suicide occurs when both these elements are present, and consequently suicide is frequent in the immature 'oral type', who tends to be over-demanding and easily frustrated in personal relationships;

[1] F. Wertham, op. cit.

[2] 'Differential Diagnosis of types of Suicides,' *Archiv. Neurol. and Psychiat.*, 1936

as well as in the violent psychopathic type, whose super-ego and propensity for self-punishment may not always be so vestigial as surface appearances suggest. Suicide may also occur in persons who appear outwardly as paragons of rectitude, since these are the people with hyper-sensitive consciences who repress their feelings of hatred, and would sooner destroy themselves than allow any open expression of their murderous impulses.

In the examples so far described the aggressive motivations were conscious and easily identified. However, if Freudian theory is correct, there should be many more cases motivated by unconscious or repressed hostility, and this would only become apparent on close clinical examination by an expert observer. On the psycho-analytic interpretation just outlined, individuals who cannot love without at the same time feeling irritated or enraged by the object of their attachment are particularly liable to suicide through the turning inwards of their frustrated emotions. In such cases, however, the underlying hostility is usually concealed behind a surface display of affectionate concern. Zilborg,[1] in a classic paper on the psychopathology of suicide, quoted some instructive examples of this sort. In one case, a married man fell into a suicidal depression while mourning the death of his baby son. In his misery he despaired of being able to support his large family and let slip the remark 'one less mouth to feed'. After several determined attempts at suicide he received some psychotherapy in the course of which he revealed extremely ambivalent attitudes to all his family. In spite of superficial appearances to the contrary, he had never loved anyone unreservedly, and actually resented and wanted to be rid of his children.

Most investigators who have interested themselves in the psychodynamics of seriously suicidal individuals have arrived at similar conclusions on the importance of repressed hostility. In an interesting study of attempted suicides in Sweden, which country has a notably high suicide rate, Hendin found that in women many cases were associated with frustrated rage against emotionally cold or deserting husbands.[2] The writer traced this phenomenon to child-rearing practices, whereby

[1] ibid.
[2] 'Suicide in Sweden,' *Psychiatric Quarterly*, 1962

early separation from mother, and an early assumption of independence on the part of the child, are positively encouraged, while the outward expression of emotion in temper or tears is rather rigorously suppressed. This frustrating upbringing favours the development of an aloof, unloving type of personality which brings about frequent emotional disappointments in martial relationships, and frequent suicide. In neighbouring Denmark, Hendin found that childhood dependence on the mother was actively fostered, with the consequence that the dependency needs of adults were especially marked, and therefore the deaths or desertions of marital partners were felt very acutely, and were liable to provoke suicide.[1] In Denmark, however, suicidal patients were much less overtly destructive or aggressive, although the covertly aggressive motive of arousing guilt in others through one's own suffering was not uncommon.

Karl Menninger[2] was one of the first to emphasize that inward directed aggression might take many other forms than actual suicide. He suggested that the self-destructive behaviour of alcoholics and drug addicts, the self-punishing effects of neurotic invalidism, the criminal's compulsive repetition of the same anti-social act until detection and imprisonment inevitably ensue, the hypochondriac's eagerness for unnecessary and mutilating surgery, the dangerous psycho-somatic effects of frustrated rage (which may precipitate organic cardio-vascular disease), and the seemingly purposive way in which some accident-prone individuals take risks and court disaster, all provide examples of reactions psychologically equivalent to suicidal attempts. In these instances of supposedly attenuated or chronic suicide the unconscious need for punishment is sometimes more persistent and more obvious to others than in examples of sudden self-destruction.

While consideration of such questions might establish connections between murder-suicide incidents and more familiar kinds of behaviour, an attempt to deal with all of these topics would involve too great a digression from the main theme. However, an example of alleged substitute suicide of special significance in criminology, which cannot be passed over

[1] 'Suicide in Denmark,' *Psychiatric Quarterly*, 1960
[2] op. cit.

without some mention, is the extraordinary propensity for bringing about their own downfall and punishment which some criminals display. Franz Alexander has traced the close analogy which exists between this unconscious need for punishment and the neurotic patient's unconscious need to perpetuate his unpleasant symptoms.[1] Whereas the healthy person's conduct conforms without much effort to some consistent pattern of social behaviour, the neurotic seems to be pushed and pulled in contrary directions. In psycho-analytic terminology, his own instinctual impulses are at war with his super-ego. The symptoms he produces, although superficially nonsensical, actually fulfil a definite function. On the one hand, they provide a disguised satisfaction for forbidden impulses. On the other hand, through the suffering and punishment involved in the unpleasant aspect of the symptoms, they relieve guilt feelings and pave the way for further transgressions. Just as the child who thinks he has been punished unfairly feels less guilty afterwards about breaking parental rules, so the neurotic (whose mental processes reproduce infantile reactions), having brought suffering upon himself through his symptoms, thereafter feels freer to indulge in fantasies that transgress the rules of the super-ego. One of the clearest examples of this process occurs in obsessional neurotics, in whom the aggressive and sexual motives behind their symptoms, as well as their self-punishing quality are often very thinly disguised indeed. Thus, patients may complain of obsessively repetitive obscene thoughts, or frightening ideas of harming their loved ones, while at the same time their lives are tyrannized by germ phobias and their hands are red-raw from washing compulsions. The obsessional neurotic plays out his conflicts internally in symptom formation and fantasy, but the neurotic criminal releases his aggressive urges externally in anti-social acts and relies on the reactions of authority to supply the guilt-relieving punishment which emboldens him to commit further crimes.

To illustrate the neurotic basis of certain crimes Alexander quotes the case of Karl, a young man who shot his girl-friend in a hotel bedroom, intending to kill himself afterwards, but lost courage and called the police instead, thus fortunately

[1] F. Alexander and H. Staub, *The Criminal, the Judge and the Public*, Revised Edition, 1956

bringing his mental processes under psycho-analytic scrutiny. In brief, it appeared that Karl had an unresolved Oedipal fixation upon his deceased mother, which had up till recently had the effect of making him aggressive and critical towards women and preventing him from forming anything more than short-lived, promiscuous sexual relations with them. When his father, from whom he had been estranged, remarried, he became reconciled, visited their home every day, and paid great attention to his step-mother, who was in poor health. When his father made some mild comment about this, he left their home in a rage, and shortly afterwards started his first real love affair with a woman who bore a close physical resemblance to his step-mother. This unconscious acting-out of incest wishes both gratified his instincts and aroused his guilt. The woman filled her fantasy role all too neatly. She was well-off and Karl was impecunious, which led to her providing for him more like a mother than a girl-friend. As she was officially engaged to another, their liaison had the added excitement of something forbidden. They both recognized that she would have to marry the other man eventually, as otherwise her parents would cut off her money. One day she suggested that they could remain lovers after she was married. This comment, like the father's comment about his attentions to his step-mother, by arousing his unconscious sense of guilt, provoked in Karl an irrational and disproportionate emotional reaction. He found the suggestion unthinkably immoral, and threatened suicide, whereupon the girl said she wished to die with him, thus providing 'simultaneously a gratification of their erotic wishes and a self-imposed punishment for this gratification'.[1] Owing to Karl's incest fantasies being repressed and unconscious, he displayed remarkable lack of remorse or guilt following the shooting. Indeed, he produced a revealing rationalization, saying that he had wanted to spare his sweetheart from an unhappy marriage such as his brother's, whose wife was lazy, profligate and unfaithful. This would have made sense only if his sweetheart were also bad. Actually, Karl had discovered in his mistress the hated, forbidden part of his own instinctual drives, so that killing her would in effect be destroying his own bad self, a deed meriting self-congratulation rather than

[1] ibid., p. 158

remorse. Freud said that suicide represents a substitute for the murder of another person. Alexander suggests that 'the reverse is also true, i.e. that many *neurotic murders* represent *disguised suicides*'.[1]

This particular example has been mentioned on account of the direct relevance of the case to murder-suicides, but the self-same psychological process of punishment seeking to assuage unconscious guilt has been suggested as the basis of all kinds of crime. Whenever the offender does stupid things which increase the likelihood of detection (e.g. signing his own name when giving a dud cheque to a stranger, or carrying out some compulsive ritual in a burgled house which stamps the crime with his personal mark) one suspects a neurotic motive. It is an open question how far this theory fits the general run of criminals, most of whom strike the observer as robustly free from the anxiety, indecisiveness, and contradictory behaviour which are the usual signs of unconscious conflict. However, one cannot always tell from superficial appearances. Without the further insight provided by psycho-analytic explanation the case of Karl would have appeared a commonplace aggressive outburst by a somewhat unfeeling and impulsive young man of defective super-ego.

Another criminological phenomenon that has been interpreted as a suicide equivalent is the traffic accident caused by aggressive and 'suicidal' driving. In a recent study of particular interest Selzer and Payne examined a group of male psychiatric patients undergoing psychotherapy in the Veterans' Readjustment Centre of the University of Michigan.[2] They compared patients who were known to have, or who admitted having, suicidal preoccupations with non-suicidal patients, and discovered that the former group had a significantly greater incidence of automobile accidents, although the two groups were similar in socio-economic background and driving experience. A half of the men were alcoholics, and they contributed a disproportionately large number of accidents, but this was true of both the suicidal and non-suicidal groups. An even greater contrast was evident between suicidal and

[1] ibid., p. 177

[2] 'Automobile Accidents, Suicide and Alcoholism,' *Proc. 3rd Internat. Conf. on Alcohol and Road Traffic*, 1963

non-suicidal than between alcoholic and non-alcoholic. In the authors' opinion these findings suggested that many persons with self-destructive inclinations may attempt to destroy or injure themselves in car accidents. They commented that 'the automobile may also constitute a special enticement to the aggressive and vengeful feelings present in many would-be suicides' since 'more conventional modes of suicide do not offer as dramatic an opportunity for the gratification of destructive and aggressive impulses'. They also pointed out that the use of the automobile for self-destruction or injury is rarely perceived consciously, either by the driver or the public, as amounting to an attempted suicide.

These findings in regard to suicidal impulses complement other research findings on the influence of aggressive responses in producing traffic accidents and traffic offences. In a celebrated psychiatric study of Canadian taxi drivers, Tillman and Hobbs compared groups of men with high and low accident records respectively.[1] The former group displayed many anti-social traits, frequently had police records for offences other than traffic regulation infringements, and generally showed marked aggression, intolerance of authority, unstable family background, frequent changes of employment, frequent contact with social agencies, and promiscuous sexual habits. After many hours of riding in their cars, the investigators concluded that the driving of a typical accident-prone man was marked by 'the same tendency of aggressiveness, impulsiveness and lack of thought for others and the disrespect for authority that was noted in his personal life'. The recent British study by Terence Willett of drivers convicted of serious traffic offences[2] – most of whom came to Court as a result of accidents – confirmed the existence of many aggressively anti-social and criminal characters among them. Over three-quarters of those convicted of the most serious offences (causing death by dangerous driving or driving while disqualified) had criminal records. In 77 cases out of his total sample of 653 offenders, Willett found either a previous conviction for violence or clear evidence of violent or aggressive behaviour in connection with the incident itself. It is strong evidence in support of the theory

[1] 'The accident-prone and automobile driver,' *Amer. Journ. Psychiatry*, 1949
[2] *Criminal on the Road*, London, 1964

linking suicidal tendency with aggressive personality that both these factors are found to be important in the production of road accidents. An actual case in which traffic accident, murder and suicide were all closely linked has been quoted already.[1]

(2) *Motivations seen in the Murder-Suicide Sample*

In the present survey, the murder-suicides by sane offenders showed, on the whole, less evidence of ambivalent love-hate motives than some of the crimes by psychotic individuals. Not that the motives of resentment, jealousy or despair observed among the insane differ in kind from those experienced by normal individuals, but rather that the insane person experiences them intensively and sometimes inappropriately, and yields to them impulsively. Since the sample was selected on the basis of the offenders' suicide, which in itself indicates a high degree of desperation and personal involvement, opportunity does not arise to make this kind of contrast between the motives of the sane and insane groups. However, a closely related question can be asked, namely how often in these cases of murder-suicide is the impulse primarily directed towards self-destruction, with a third party involved only incidentally, and how often is the impulse primarily murderous, with the suicide an after-thought, provoked perhaps by guilt feelings or fear of punishment? And if this distinction can be made, are the murder-suicides by the insane more often primarily self-destructive?

Norwood East has pointed out that the need to distinguish between acts primarily murderous, but followed by suicide, and crimes primarily suicidal, but extended to involve a third party, applies equally to crimes committed by sane and insane persons. He wrote, 'The fact that 38% of those suspected of murder commit suicide is no evidence for or against insanity ... In some circumstances suicide may be preferable to the indignity of judicial execution or the suffering involved in serving a life imprisonment.'[2] The idea that these suicides are frequently independent of the murders which preceded them was also put forward by Hoffman[3] in the course of an attack

---

[1] See p. 78
[2] W. Norwood East, *Society and the Criminal*, (1949), p. 273
[3] *The Homicide Problem* (Newark, 1925), p. 106

on the United States government for 'gross neglect' in allowing substantial numbers of murderers and other offenders to escape punishment by committing suicide in prison on the eve of their trial. Several different lines of evidence all pointed to self-destruction as the prime motive in the majority of the murder-suicide cases. In the total sample, 22 of the 148 offenders (that is 15%) had made previous suicidal attempts. This figure, which may be considered a measure of suicidal tendency, actually exceeds the figure for the incidence of previous attempts in the case of suicides not associated with murder. Thus, in his study of London suicides, Sainsbury reported previous attempts in 9% of cases,[1] and Parnell and Skottowe at Oxford 11%.[2]

Another feature strongly suggesting unambiguous suicidal intentions in these cases was that in most instances the murder and the suicide took place virtually simultaneously, whereas one might have expected some time to elapse between the two events if the suicides arose secondarily, as a result of the development of remorse or the fear of punishment. Of the 78 offenders in the main sample, 39 used gas for the killing, and most of these lay down to die with their victims, and indeed some may have expired before their victims. Thirteen offenders killed themselves in some other place than they had murdered, but in most of these cases the time interval was not more than a few hours. Thus, 3 offenders walked out and drowned themselves almost immediately after committing murder, one of them unsuccessfully attempting suicide by other means first. One offender spent some hours visiting the victim's family before killing himself, and another spent some time in a cinema. In only two instances was the time gap considerable, one being the case of the offender who killed himself 3 days later while in custody (Case 59), and the other being the man who killed himself 5 days later when the police were about to catch up with him (Case 12).

Of the offenders who died in the same place as their victims, only two delayed their suicide by more than a day. In one of these cases (Case 2), the two bodies were found together, death having been due to taking drugs. The fact that a time lag of about 24 hours had apparently elapsed between the

[1] op. cit.   [2] op. cit.

deaths was largely responsible for the verdict of murder-suicide rather than double suicide. In the other case (Case 33), a family murder by a mentally ill husband, a day elapsed during which the murderer wrote pathetic descriptions of what had transpired before finally taking his own life.

A third piece of evidence bearing upon the level of aggression manifest in these cases arose from the methods of suicide chosen by the offenders. Supposing that a substantial proportion of cases arose from motives of hostility or rage against the victim (these emotions being subsequently turned against the self according to the psychological processes previously described) then one might expect a higher incidence of violent methods of self-destruction than in an ordinary series of suicides. This expectation was not borne out by the data. Capstick,[1] analysing methods of suicide in 881 cases in Wales in 1951–5, found that women used 'passive' methods, such as gas, barbiturate or other forms of poisoning, whereas men more often chose 'active' methods, such as cutting, hanging, shooting and drowning. Table 18 shows the comparative incidence of active and passive methods in the present sample and in Capstick's study.

It would appear that there was no substantial difference between the two samples in the methods of suicide chosen by males, but that the females in the murder-suicide series had an even stronger preference for passive methods than ordinary female suicides. This may have been due to the predominantly urban situation of the murder-suicide sample, with an associated ease of access to coal gas, or to the obvious suitability of coal gas for the painless extermination of young children. But whatever the reason, the suicides in the present survey were no more violent in method than in a series of ordinary suicides.

Finally, in the main sample of murder-suicide offenders, a significant number were in poor or failing physical health, and in some cases (e.g. Cases 5, 14 and 68) this seemed to constitute an important motive for the crime. In this respect the sample resembled any series of ordinary suicides in which, as has often been pointed out, failing health or painful disease in the elderly, especially the elderly man, constitutes a very common precipitating motive.

[1] *Brit. Med. Journ.*, 1960

All of these points favour the view that the majority of murder-suicide offenders felt driven to suicide by illness or distressing circumstances, and that the victim was usually an innocent party, involved only by virtue of a close relationship with the suicidal offender. However, there were notable exceptions, particularly among those described as 'criminal types', psychopaths and paranoid cases, but as these have been cited fully in previous sections they need not be repeated here. Motives of sexual jealousy, rage following personal rejections, and imagined grievances of various kinds featured prominently in these cases.

To answer the second question posed, whether a primary suicidal motivation was commoner in the offenders considered 'insane', the factors mentioned above are shown in Table 19 in relation to the two groups of sane and insane offenders. The case histories were scrutinized for evidence of manifest hostility towards the victim having constituted a prime motive, or for evidence that the offender was closely identified with his victim and felt that in killing himself he could not leave the other to live on alone. Rather surprisingly, a history of previous suicidal attempts was commoner, and indications that the prime motive was extended suicide was almost as common, in the sane as in the insane groups. Manifestly hostile motives were quite evident in some of the 'insane' as well as in some of the 'sane' offenders. Typical examples in which murderous aggression appeared a prime motive were Case 54 (p. 51) – the rejected lover who shot his girl-friend dead, leaving behind a suicide note full of recriminations for the way she had treated him – and Case 60 (p. 86), the leucotomized mental patient who killed his prostitute friend because he was jealous and suspected that she wanted him only for his money. On the whole, overtly hostile motives were more in evidence among the 'sane' than the 'insane' offenders, but this may have been a consequence of the fact that there was a larger proportion of men among the 'sane' offenders and men display overt aggression more readily than women. In Table 19 it has not been possible to classify all of the murder-suicide cases as motivated primarily either by hostile or by suicidal impulses, since in some instances information was too scanty and in others the apparent motives were very mixed. So far as the comparison goes it suggests that most of the murder-suicide incidents were of the extended suicide variety without evidence of overt hostility towards the victim. The minority of cases in which aggression directed against the victim constituted a prime motive were associated with the sane more than the insane and with male offenders more than female offenders.

X

Social Determinants of Murder or Suicide

IF THE theory that suicide represents a form of thwarted murder applies to a sufficient proportion of cases, one could expect evidence for this in the statistics of violent deaths. Thus, in cultures in which violence towards others is especially taboo, one would expect a relatively high proportion of violent deaths to be suicidal rather than homicidal.

The relation between the statistics of murder and those of suicide, and the overlap between the two, have long been of particular interest to criminologists on account of a theory, originating in the nineteenth century in the writings of such authorities as Morselli[1] and Ferri,[2] to the effect that suicide and homicide represent alternative effects of a common cause which finds an outlet sometimes in one form and sometimes in the other. At periods when the response to social miseries often takes a self-destructive form, the number of murderous attacks on others would be expected to be correspondingly low. The early criminologists attempted to demonstrate that homicide and suicide incidence vary inversely, so that age groups, races, areas, social classes, or temporal periods associated with a high suicide rate tend to be also associated with a low homicide rate.

From its first inception, however, the theory that homicide and suicide are complementary was seriously challenged, notably by Tarde,[3] Durkheim[4] and later Halbwachs.[5] Their criticisms applied both to the data and to the interpretations. They pointed out many exceptions to the inverse rule. For

---

[1] *Suicide* (New York, 1882)   [2] *L'Omicidio-Suicidio* (Turin, 1892)
[3] *Penal Philosophy*, translation (Boston, 1912)   [4] op. cit.
[5] *Les Causes du Suicide* (Paris, 1930)

instance, in most countries women have a relatively low suicide rate as well as a low homicide rate. Furthermore both homicide and suicide show simultaneous seasonal increases in the Spring. Sometimes the suicide rate fluctuates drastically without any corresponding change in homicide rates. Even admitting a certain statistical relationship, this does not necessarily imply any direct causal link, since many social statistics fluctuate in unison as a result perhaps of changing community circumstances, seasonal influences, migration, and a host of other factors that have no specific connection with the particular item under consideration.

A rough idea of the relationship between murder and suicide can be obtained by comparing different countries in regard to incidence of suicide and self-inflicted injuries on the one hand and homicide and acts of war on the other, both sets of data being published by the World Health Organization. It can be seen from Table 20 that, contrary to theoretical assumptions, some of the countries with high homicide rates, such as Finland and Japan, also have high suicide rates. The position is still further complicated by the fact that whereas females contribute negligibly to the homicide statistics they occupy a varying proportion of the suicide statistics. Suicide rates for males and females respectively are 26·6 and 18·9 in Japan; 14·2 and 8·9 in Denmark; 16·6 and 4·7 in the United States. Indeed, the general picture of suicide rates is one of extreme and surprising contrasts. In any one society, grouping according to social class, marital condition, age, sex and racial origin all yield very different rates, but no one of these factors has a preponderant effect under all circumstances. For example, although females almost always have a lower suicide rate than males of the same age and culture, elderly Japanese females have a suicide rate over a hundred times that of young American coloured males.[1]

A larger table prepared by A. L. Wood, showed the homicide and suicide rates of 36 countries, based on average rates for years 1951 to 1956, as given in the United Nations *Demographic Yearbooks*, but eliminating years in which a country was at war or in revolution.[2] The median homicide rate was 1·7, the median suicide rate was 8·5, and a suggestive association

---

[1] J. P. Gibbs in Merton and Nisbet [Eds.], *Contemporary Social Problems* (New York, 1961, Ch. 5, Table 10)   [2] op. cit., Table 16, p. 55

emerged between high suicide rates and low homicide rates, and vice versa. This result, reproduced as Table 21, would seem to lend support to the inverse relationship theory, notwithstanding the many exceptions and complicating factors.

A word of caution is necessary here. In comparing suicide rates in different countries, one has to allow for the fact that standards of reporting and recording may vary considerably. It is often said that in Catholic countries, in which religious principles operate to produce particularly strong condemnation of suicide, there will be some reluctance to record a verdict of suicide except in absolutely indisputable cases. In spite of such considerations, however, the contrasts are very striking between England and places like Jamaica and the Latin American States, where suicide is a rarity and homicide relatively common-place. There are also countries, such as Finland and the United States, which have a relatively large incidence of both homicide and suicide. In these examples, the differences are so substantial and persistent that they could hardly be due entirely to varying standards of reporting.

In spite of the complexity of the personal and social factors that determine the patterns of murder and homicide, and the likelihood that different types of murder or suicide have altogether different causes, investigators still persist in the search for some meaningful relationship which holds true for a sufficient number of cases to produce identifiable trends in the statistics of incidence. Durkheim himself, although he attacked Ferri's views, argued forcibly in favour of discernible connections between suicide rates and social conditions. He distinguished three types. *Egotistic* suicide occurred in exces-sively individualistic personalities who declined to conform to commonly accepted roles, living according to their own preferences and ideals instead of being fully integrated into society. This explained the fact that members of religious and political minorities, as well as unmarried persons, had above average suicide rates. The less common *altruistic* type occurred in precisely opposite circumstances, consisting of individuals sacrificing themselves to society out of a sense of duty or honour. Defeated soldiers killing themselves to preserve the honour of the Corps or to avoid bringing shame on their families, and widows in India allowing themselves to be burned on their husband's funeral pyre, were examples of this kind. Lastly, *anomic* suicide arose from a disorganization of society itself, from a loosening of traditional rules and constraints, leaving individuals free to act upon their own impulses. Economic crises, having the effect of unsettling established norms through a swift movement of individuals from one social class to another; industrialization, with resulting migration to unfamiliar places and customs; and the personal crisis of widowhood or divorce, with consequent loosening of domestic regularities, all tended to be accompanied by increased suicide rates.

Although difficult to define, anomie or social disorganization has proved a popular concept in sociological research. 'Anomic' urban areas, characterized by extreme lack of social cohesion, in which the population consists of drifting, rootless persons owing allegiance to no particular cultural standards, are known to be identified with a high incidence of many forms of social deviation including poverty, broken families, promiscuity and crime. Durkheim correctly predicted a high rate of suicide under such conditions. He pointed out, however, that not all poor communities are in a state of anomie. If the members of a backward rural community accept their poverty-stricken position as a fact of nature (as did most of the peasants of Southern Ireland and Calabria in Durkheim's day) they are not in a state of anomie and the people will avoid the disappointments resulting from futile attempts to break the bounds of social restraint, and so will have a low suicide rate. In contrast, persons whose social status changes, either downward through economic depression, or upward through business prosperity, experience an imbalance between their ambitions and desires and the social constraints within which they must live. The person who has sunk cannot adjust to unaccustomed limitations, the person who has risen imagines all restraints gone and soon finds himself disappointed. In either case, liability to suicide increases considerably. As another example, Durkheim refers to matrimony which, by encouraging regularity and restraint in the sexual sphere, shields the married, while leaving the single and divorced, who live in a state of sexual anomie, especially prone to suicide. Durkheim goes so far as to point out that on his theory there may be no antithesis but actually a parallelism between suicide and homicide under certain circumstances since, 'Anomy, in fact, begets a state of exasperation and irritated weariness which may turn against the person himself or another according to circumstances . . .'[1]

Durkheim's theories were largely speculative and intuitive. He was careless about defining his categories, and produced little in the way of empirical findings in support of his views, but his work has considerable historical significance because it has been the starting point of many more recent sociological researches. A serious attempt to formulate the Durkheim hypotheses more scientifically and to test them with reference to the observed fluctuations in murder rates and suicide rates in the United States, was made by Henry and Short.[2] These investigators noted, as had Durkheim, that suicide was more frequent in groups of high social status (men more than women, whites more than negroes, officers more than enlisted men) and more frequent among isolated persons (e.g. the unmarried, divorced, widowed and aged). They suggested that the common factor was the degree to which behaviour was regulated by external restraints rather than individual choice. This would be high in those of low status as well as those living in intimate relations with others, so that in such cases the aggressions aroused when things go wrong would tend to be directed against others. Those who feel more responsible for their own decisions, and those who lead solitary, individualistic lives, having only themselves to blame, are relatively more likely to commit suicide: 'When behaviour is freed from external restraint, the self must bear the responsibility for frustration. Others cannot be blamed since others were not involved in the determination of behaviour. Under these conditions, other-oriented expression of the resultant aggression fails to be legitimized.'[3] On the same argument, contrary trends could be predicted for homicide, white persons having smaller rates than negroes since white persons are less constrained and more self-determined, and old persons having a smaller homicide rate than young ones (since they are more isolated and individualistic). Broadly speaking the facts conformed to these expectations. The one striking exception was

[1] op. cit., p. 357   [2] *Suicide and Homicide* (Glencoe, Ill., 1954)
[3] ibid., p. 103

that of the contrast between the sexes. On the supposition that women are of lower status and more constrained, the theory predicts that they would have a lower suicide rate and a higher homicide rate than men. While the former holds true, the latter contradicts the well-known fact that crimes of violence are relatively rarely committed by women. Incidentally, Henry and Short also argue in another context that old retired people are relatively lower in status than younger working people, a factor which should make for old people having a higher homicide rate and a lower suicide rate, which is plainly contradictory to the facts.

Henry and Short also investigated the fluctuations in homicide and suicide rates which accompany economic changes. They found a consistent negative correlation between an economic index of industrial activity and the U.S. suicide rates. That is to say, in times of prosperity suicide rates tended to fall, and in times of depression to rise, as might be expected if suicide rates provide an index of social frustration and stress. They also found that the correlation was much closer for higher status groups, who obviously had more to lose in a business depression than those who were already at the bottom rung of the ladder and would therefore be only slightly affected. They found that the statistics of homicide and crimes of violence (aggravated assault) in the United States generally fluctuated in the opposite direction to the suicide rate, and correlated positively with the business index. Particularly noticeable was the fall in crimes of violence during periods of depression. This seems paradoxical, since one might expect increasing social frustration to provoke an increase in both murder and suicide. Henry and Short suggested that the explanation lay in the different response to frustration in high status and low status groups, the former choosing suicide when things go wrong, the latter blaming and attacking others. During a depression the low status categories, who are responsible for most of the violent crimes, actually experience a relative improvement in status, as those formerly much better off swiftly lose their advantage. This reduction in the disparity of wealth and status should effectively reduce frustration, and hence lower the homicide rate, but not the suicide rate, since that is an upper class reaction, and the upper classes are being heavily frustrated during economic depression. The hypothesis received some confirmation from the contrasting trends of the two races, negroes (low status) showing a reduction in homicide during depression, and whites (higher status) an increase. Whether these sociological hypotheses can be applied to cultures greatly different from our own remains to be seen, but at least one sociological analysis of homicide and suicide in an Eastern country has been reported, that is A. L. Wood's survey of Ceylon.[1] His report makes difficult reading, owing to some confusion between the statement of theory and the presentation of data in support. Nevertheless, Wood made a number of interesting observations that conformed with the hypotheses that stress or frustration promotes both suicidal and homicidal aggressions, and that stress affecting the economically deprived masses will favour homicide rather than suicide. A gradual social change, in which the upper classes, formerly insulated from the strains of achievement by inherited wealth and secure status, find themselves exposed to a newer system of economic and social mobility, has been accompanied by a steadily increasing suicide rate, the incidence of 80 per 100,000 of population in 1957 representing twice the incidence at the turn of the century. Homicide incidence, on the other hand, apart from temporary fluctuations, remained much the same as half a century ago.[2] Economic depression was found to have a different association with homicide and suicide from that reported by Henry and Short in the United States. The connection between suicide rates and the business cycle was almost negligible. However, during the years of severe economic recession associated with the last world war, both homicide rates and the incidence of crimes against property rose sharply.[3] Wood noted that the section of the population most prone to homicide, the working classes of the Maritime regions, was in fact the group affected worst by the depression. These people, though poor were not the most socially depressed in absolute terms, but they had experienced great changes in the process of urbanization, and been harshly confronted with the class contrasts and social aspirations of the big towns without as yet achieving full integrations into city life. Their livelihood depended upon trade continuing normally.

[1] op. cit.   [2] ibid., Table 18, pp. 57 and 106   [3] ibid., fig. II, p. 81

Henry and Short recognized that two sets of factors were at work; the first (which they identified with various stresses and social frustrations) by provoking aggression might be expected to generate both homicide and suicide. The second set of factors determined the choice between homicide and suicide, that is between outward or inward directed violence. Gold, in an attempt to make more accurate assessments of these factors, pointed out that the crude incidence rates of murder and suicide may both be presumed to reflect levels of frustration, and that a better measure of the degree to which one of these responses occurs in preference to the other would be the proportion of suicides in the combined incidence of both murders and suicides. This he called the suicide-murder ratio.[1]

Use of this ratio clarifies Durkheim's proposition about high suicide and high homicide rates occurring simultaneously in certain circumstances. In poor areas of drifting population, in which social stresses are acute and many individuals live under isolated conditions in bed-sitting rooms, suicide is common, but so also is homicide, the net effect being that the suicide-murder ratio remains small, as is typical of low status groups. Higher status groups may not always show larger absolute numbers of suicides, but they are likely to show a consistently higher suicide-murder ratio.

On Henry and Short's hypothesis, the suicide-murder ratio is small among low status groups because they are subject to numerous external constraints and can therefore find numerous external targets for their aggression. Gold suggested an alternative interpretation, namely that the degree to which the culture of the group permitted physical aggression was the more fundamental factor. Lower class groups tend to express their emotions physically, and to control their children by physical punishments, whereas middle class ideology favours verbal over physical expression, and psychological over physical methods of child discipline. This assumption leads to the same prediction as Henry and Short with regard to social class, the lower classes having the lower suicide-murder ratio. On the question of sex differences, however, Gold's hypothesis predicts correctly a higher suicide-murder ratio for females (in

[1] 'Suicide, Homicide and Aggression,' *Amer. Journ. Sociol.*, 1958

spite of their supposed status inferiority), since physical punishments are used less with girls than boys, and physical aggression is less acceptable among women than among men. Gold's theory also predicted correctly a greater suicide-murder ratio in urban than in rural areas, on the assumption that the more complexly organized urban dwellers would place a high value on co-operation and the inhibition of external aggression.

The mention of cultural standards of aggressive behaviour leads directly to the psychological factors associated with child training and personality development which Henry and Short considered equally important in determining the mode of expressing aggression. Following Freudian terminology, persons of strong super-ego, who have *internalized* parental precepts very thoroughly during infancy, are likely throughout their lives to conform meticulously to society's rules, to feel guilty about even minor infractions, and to blame themselves and turn their aggression upon themselves rather than against others. In contrast, those of weak super-ego, otherwise described as immature or psychopathic, are impulsive and unrestrained in behaviour, lack guilt feelings, and blame and attack others and not themselves. Investigations of the family background of offenders, and of the effect of child-rearing practices upon personality development, suggest that parental firmness and consistency, within a context of affection and concern, favours the development of a strong super-ego. On the other hand, parental rejection and lack of love appears to interfere with the processes whereby the child identifies himself with his parents' values, and favours poor super-ego development, regardless of the types of discipline enforced. Neglect and laxness in child training may have a similar effect, even when the parents are not hostile.

The child-rearing practices of the middle classes are more likely to favour strong super-ego development than those of the lower classes. Since aggression is fostered by frustration, severe and restrictive child-rearing methods will encourage aggression, but if the originator of the frustration is a parent to whom he is strongly attached, his main source of 'love and nurturance' in fact, he will feel guilty and turn his aggression inwards. If the severe parent is not a loving provider, then the child's aggression remains overt and externally directed.

On the basis of this general theory, Henry and Short made the prediction that a person who commits an aggressive act against a spouse, for instance, is particularly liable to strong guilt feelings, since he has attacked a prime source of 'love and nurturance'. The fact that divorced persons are more liable to suicide than the widowed is consistent with their theory that those who have lost a spouse through their own actions will feel more angry with themselves than those who have lost a spouse from external causes. Murderers who have destroyed a source of love and nurturance will be especially prone to subsequent suicide. Henry and Short suggest that this hypothesis would be favoured if an unusual degree of positive attachment of offender to victim were to be found in those cases of murder which are followed by the suicide of the aggressor. On Gold's theory, one might make the prediction that murder-suicide sequence would be commoner in female than in male murderers, on the argument that women are less tolerant of aggression and would feel more guilty after having committed a murderous act.

These theories about personality and class differences and their relation to the expression of aggression could be used to predict various points on which murderers who kill themselves would be likely to differ from murderers in general. On the assumption that the murder-suicide incidence is an example of aggression partially deflected inwards, whereas the ordinary murder consists of violence entirely directed outwards, one would expect the former group of offenders to display some of the qualities of a better-developed super-ego. Thus, compared with ordinary murderers, they should be more middle class, more respectable and conformist in their behaviour, relatively free from histories of previous criminal convictions, more likely to have acted on desperate provocation than from criminal intent, and more likely to be persons of mature years or members of the female sex. As will be recalled from the conclusions of Chapter III, the comparison of the murder and murder-suicide samples yielded differences on all these points in the direction expected on the hypothesis that murder-suicide offenders would come from groups in which externally directed violence is more rigorously proscribed. These differences were still present, and still in the same direction, after eliminating the insane cases, so they could not be accounted for by peculiarities in the class distribution of depressive psychosis. The differences were well marked notwithstanding the evidence that the murder-suicide offenders included some highly aggressive individuals. Possibly younger and lower class males who are homicidally aggressive tend to concentrate their violence more against others, whereas middle-class aggressives of mature age also attack themselves.

A prediction that murder-suicide incidents would tend to be confined to persons acting under extreme pressure or provocation follows from the hypothesis that such crimes are the work of offenders who ordinarily keep their violence in check. In fact, there were hardly any unprovoked killings of strangers among the murder-suicides, although these were not uncommon among the ordinary murders. There were many unprovoked killings of children by their parents, however, but these were mostly the result of serious mental illness, which could be regarded as one form of 'pressure'. It was certainly true that most of the killings of adult victims by sane offenders took place in circumstances of extreme personal frustration, such as long-standing marital disputes, or broken love affairs, and that almost invariably a strong emotional tie bound offender and victim together in their fatal situation. One might argue further that in countries with a high homicide rate, in which cultural proscriptions against externally directed violence are rather low and inward-turning aggression is relatively rare, that the proportion of murders followed by suicide will be small. This, in fact, appears to be the general trend.

The fact that the suicide-to-murder ratio in England is relatively large[1] supports the theory that the cultural barriers against murderous violence are very high in this country, so that frustrated individuals are more likely to turn their aggression on themselves than to kill someone else. On this theory one would expect that even among those who go so far as to commit murder, many would have contemplated or attempted suicide previously as a preferred solution to their difficulties, and many more would only go so far as to kill another when they had also decided to die themselves. This was precisely in accord with the present findings. In England,

[1] See Tables 1 and 20

one murder suspect commits suicide for every two brought to trial, and many murderers were found to have made attempts to kill themselves before they attacked anyone else. Moreover, among ordinary murderers who remained alive and came to trial, a substantial number were essentially similar in character to the murder-suicide cases, that is individuals driven to distraction and despair by mental illness or intolerable situations. The observation that English murderers brought to trial less frequently have a criminal record, and are not so predominantly lower class, than in some American studies, points to the same trend. The trigger-happy killer, with no inhibitions about attacking others, and no desire to harm himself, was a comparative rarity in English murderers. Such criminals are more typical of places like the South of the United States, where among certain classes, especially lower class negroes, violence against others is more expected, and the suicide-to-murder ratio is particularly low.

Somewhat different predictions follow if, instead of emphasizing that the aggression in murder-suicide has been partially deflected inwards, one takes the line that the level of aggression in such cases must have been extraordinarily high. Durkheim, for example,[1] argues that if suicide and homicide provide a violent-natured individual with alternative outlets for his aggression, then one would expect arrested murderers, whose violence can no longer find external expression, to resort to suicide, but, as has been noted, this rarely happens in practice. On the same line of argument, however, one might have predicted that there could be found in the histories of murder-suicide offenders other instances of explosive aggression, in the shape of previous suicidal attempts, or previous violence towards others, or both. Actually, decisive evidence on the nature of the determining factors in murder-suicides cannot be expected from the analysis of trends of total incidence. Very likely different explanations fit different categories. If the present inquiry has done nothing else it has at least shown that the indiscriminating violence of the psychopath, the despairing mother who kills her children, and the unhappy couples who decide to die together, are not to be squeezed into any single motivational theory.

[1] op. cit., p. 345

XI

Summary and Conclusions

IN so far as the sample of murder-suicide incidents proved
substantially different from the sample of ordinary murders
which are brought to Court, the findings confirmed the fallacy
of generalization about murder based solely upon tried and
convicted offenders. The most striking distinguishing features
of the murder-suicides were the large numbers of women
offenders and child victims, the very small numbers of offenders
with previous convictions, and the total absence of the young
thug who kills in the furtherance of theft or robbery. An
overlap of similar cases in both samples was noticeable,
particularly in crimes committed by women, by insane
offenders, and by murderers who subsequently attempt suicide
unsuccessfully.

From a social point of view, the murder-suicide offenders
constituted a less deviant group than the sample of ordinary
murderers. Unlike the murderers, who included an excess of
young, unmarried males, and of individuals of the lowest
social class, the murder-suicide offenders were in these respects
more representative of the general community, and the
majority of them were married and living in a conventional
family setting free from criminal associations. These differences
were in keeping with predictions based on sociological theory,
as described in Chapter X.

The psychiatric prediction that nearly all murder-suicides
would be found to have been committed by 'insane' persons
was proved wrong. The American findings of Wolfgang and
Cavan, that murder followed by suicide is rarely committed by
insane persons, was also shown to be untrue of an English
sample. In fact, one half of the offenders were considered
sufficiently abnormal to be regarded as insane or of diminished

responsibility by legal standards. This proportion was almost identical to that which was found in a comparable sample of murderers brought to trial and not acquitted. One might conclude that in both England and America murder-suicide offenders do not differ from ordinary murderers in the likelihood of insanity, and that where the likelihood is high for murderers at large it is also high for murderers who kill themselves. However, this apparent statistical equivalence is somewhat misleading, since it conceals some contrary trends. The substantial numbers of insane among the English murder-suicide offenders was partly associated with the relatively high proportion of women, and the fact that women who kill are so much more likely to be insane than male killers. Thus, taking the sexes separately, the murder-suicide offenders were actually rated as 'sane' more often than the murderers brought to trial were held to be sane by the Courts, (10 sane out of 34 murder-suicides compared with 4 out of 18 in the case of women offenders; 29 sane out of 44 compared with 78 out of 138 in the case of male offenders). This finding was contrary to expectation based on American studies by Gibbens and McDermaid and Winkler, according to which suicidal tendencies are less common in sane than insane murderers.

The fact that so many murder-suicide offenders were apparently sane did not mean that they were therefore ordinary criminals. The theory that suicide following murder is the criminal's way of avoiding punishment, which was favoured by Cavan's study, and by some of Wolfgang's cases, applied only to a very few cases in this sample. The popular stereotype of murder – the confirmed criminal who kills for gain or in the furtherance of some offence – was hardly represented at all. Compared with murders in general, the murder-suicide cases were remarkable for the preponderance of 'domestic' killings of wife, child or lover, the very type of crime which frequently leads to a finding of insanity or diminished responsibility in the case of offenders brought to trial. That this feature was not in fact associated with a higher incidence of 'insanity' in the murder-suicide offenders may have been due to excessive rigour in excluding doubtful cases from the insane category. A more probable explanation is that the 'insane' category was genuinely outnumbered by a sizeable group of persons, free from previous mental disturbance, who committed murder and suicide under pressure of collapsing physical health or impending disaster. Whereas such stresses are, in the ordinary way, precipitants of suicide but not of murder, they may become associated with murder (as a form of extended suicide) in persons who have a strong feeling for and close identification with their families. Hence the probable reason for the small proportion of murder-suicide offenders who were unmarried or living away from their families, a finding which contrasted sharply with the excess of social isolates among suicides and the excess of young unmarried persons among murderers.

The presence of a significant number of infanticides, probable death pacts, mercy-killings and possibly accidental killings among the murder-suicide cases provided another indication that many of these murder-suicide offenders were actuated by feelings of despair more than hostility. Indeed, the categories just mentioned, apart from mercy-killings, would not nowadays be called murder at all had they come to trial. It seems misleading that they should be incorporated in the official murder-rate, and unjust to the offenders' families that regardless of circumstances and mental state they should be classed legally as murderers – with all that may involve in the way of social stigma and difficulty in the disposal of property.

The Freudian theory of the interchangeability of self-directed and other-directed aggression, resulting from ambivalent love-hate attachments, received definite support from some of the murder-suicide cases, especially those in which a long and stormy emotional relationship between offenders and victims preceded the lethal outburst. Overt signs of previous hostility towards their victims, and conscious motives of jealousy, vindictiveness, and resentment, were much more frequently displayed by the male offenders, among whom the rejected lovers, jealous husbands, and violent-tempered men formed a sizeable group. The description of murder-suicides committed by men with a previous criminal record[1] brought out the important point that nearly all of these had some history of violent tendencies, although not necessarily associated with

[1] See p. 56.

convictions for crimes of violence. Among the 'sane' offenders who had no actual criminal record, violent behaviour in their domestic lives was recorded in a number of cases.[1] Among the psychopathic offenders, and those of unstable personality, uncontrolled violence was particularly prevalent.[2] Among the psychotic group, despite the preponderance of melancholics, there were some schizophrenics with hostile, paranoid delusions, and in addition some of those classed as depressives had noticeable paranoid tendencies. In fact, a significant history of violent temperament or behaviour was present in many of the male offenders, both sane and insane.

This observation, coupled with the histories of previous suicidal attempts, which were even more frequent than in a sample of ordinary suicides, suggests that at least some of the persons liable to commit murder-suicide crimes are individuals with a high level of aggression which may turn against others or against themselves according to circumstances. But their aggression is of the kind more likely to be aroused in their personal relations than to find expression in conventionally criminal acts, such as robbery or sexual assault.

The question of whether murder-suicide incidents are more closely akin to suicide than to murder is complicated by the observation that many suicides occur from motives of aggression and spite, while many murders of the domestic variety arise from feelings of despair and hopelessness. In the sample of ordinary murderers, the incidence of previous suicidal attempts was as high as in samples of persons who have committed suicide. In the main murder-suicide sample, previous suicidal attempts were even more frequent, which suggests that these offenders were unusually prone to self-destruction. In several other respects the group resembled a sample of suicides rather than a sample of murderers. In socio-economic status they had no over-representation of the lowest classes, such as occurs in ordinary murderers but not in suicides. In sex distribution, the offenders were similar to suicides and quite untypical of murderers. In age range, they were younger than suicides but older than murderers. A very much higher proportion were married than among murderers in general, and a

---

[1] e.g. Cases 46 and 47, pp. 52 and 51
[2] e.g. Cases 14, 20 and 57, pp. 85, 83 and 83

substantially higher proportion than among suicides. In weekly incidence, there was a maximum frequency at the beginning of the working week and a minimum frequency at weekends, a trend typical of suicide and contrary to that of ordinary murder. In methods of killing themselves, the murder-suicide offenders had no tendency to choose 'active' or violent modes of death more often than ordinary suicides. Almost invariably the suicide followed directly upon the commission of murder, as if in fulfilment of a single purpose. Among the offenders with identifiable mental abnormalities, depressive illness (either in the form of endogenous psychotic melancholia or of severe reactive depression) was much the commonest condition, as it is among ordinary suicides, accounting for more cases than all other diagnoses combined. The incidence of depressive types of illness was certainly higher than is the case among abnormal murderers generally, among whom schizophrenia and paranoid states are commoner. Depressive illness was especially prevalent among the female offenders, occurring in 21 out of the total of 34 women in the main murder-suicide sample, and constituting the most obvious causal factor in most instances of the killing of small children by their mothers, in the murder sample as well as the murder-suicides. There was no sharp dividing line between offenders suffering from pathological depression, and 'normal' offenders acting under pressure of misfortune. The large numbers of young married women in the murder-suicide series, untypical of ordinary suicides, was undoubtedly due to the close identification of mothers with their young children, and the consequent involvement of the children in their mothers' depressions. Contrary to medico-legal tradition, these illnesses were not especially associated with the period immediately following childbirth when women are supposed to be liable to puerperal psychosis and infanticide. On the whole, then, the results suggested that the majority of murder-suicide incidents were examples of extended suicide arising from depressing circumstances or melancholic state of mind.

The observation that the percentages of male and of female murder-suicide offenders who were considered insane was slightly less than the corresponding percentages of insane among ordinary murderers in no way altered the conclusion that a highly significant association with mental illness existed.

But mental illnesses occur thousands of times more frequently than murders followed by suicide, so one has to look for means of recognizing which mental patients present this special risk. One substantial and readily identifiable group stood out among the abnormal offenders, namely the depressed women who killed their children and themselves at the same time, usually by means of coal gas. Unfortunately, it was not possible to establish any easy rule to distinguish between the conditions of these women and those of large numbers of depressed mothers who harbour homicidal ideas without ever acting upon them. All of them were actively suicidal at the time of the killing, and it seems reasonable to suppose that if they had not had charge of young children they would have committed suicide without harming anyone else. In several cases[1] the children became involved only after the mother had failed in her initial attempts to do away with herself. All this points to the need for particular care and supervision in the psychiatric management of potentially suicidal mothers.

In the sample examined there were several incidents that might have been prevented, in which the offender had shown quite florid depressive symptoms and should have been under treatment in hospital. There were other instances which could not have been foreseen. As with unexpected suicides, the homicide incidents were apt to occur relatively early in the development of an illness, in persons who had had no previous attacks, or during phases of apparent improvement; all of which are times when relatives and others may not appreciate the gravity of the situation. From the point of view of prevention, the worst difficulty was that homicidal risk appeared not only in psychotic persons, whose confused and remote thought processes readily aroused suspicion of danger, but also in neurotic individuals, whose depth of feeling lay hidden behind a rational demeanour. Although a history of previous tendency to violence was found with significant frequency in some of the male offenders, this was not so in the case of the depressed mothers, who became dangerous only when they became suicidal. The practical conclusion to be drawn is that all depressed mothers of young children, whether or not they happen to be in a puerperal period, warrant careful

[1] e.g. Cases 7 and 16, pp. 70 and 69

individual attention; but for the sake of preventing the occasional misfortune, separation of mother and child, with the emotionally damaging and confidence-destroying effects this might have, would not be justified in the majority of cases.

Whereas the depressed mothers nearly always murdered their children out of a close sense of identification with their victims, and with no overt display of hostility, the depressed offenders who killed adult victims sometimes showed signs of irritability and ambivalence towards the victims, and occasionally showed a distinctly suspicious, paranoid trend to their thinking, such as might be expected more typically of a schizophrenic. The observations of McGrath and others that insane murderers often show a mixture of schizophrenic and depressive features, and of aggressive and altruistic motives, was shown to be true of some of the murder-suicide offenders, and confirmed that the traditional distinction between altruistically motivated melancholics and violently hostile schizophrenics is an over-simplification. The assumption that schizophrenic murderers invariably kill others but not themselves was also disproved by the presence of several such cases in the main sample. Nevertheless, on the whole, sustained and open hostility towards their victims was relatively uncommon among the depressives, who constituted the majority of the 'insane' group, and slightly more frequent among the 'sane' offenders, especially the males.

The assumption that insane murder-suicide offenders can be distinguished from the sane offenders by the method of killing, or the type of motive involved, was not confirmed by the present data.

In conclusion, it deserves to be emphasized once again, that murders followed by suicide constitute numerically so substantial a section of the murder statistics that the special characteristics of this group must have a profound effect upon any criminological analysis of English murder as a whole. Commonly accepted generalizations such as the assumption that nearly all murders are committed by men, that most insane murderers are schizophrenics, or that the lower classes predominate among offenders, hold true only so long as the crimes followed by suicide are resolutely disregarded. Moreover, consideration of the murder-suicides, apart from the intrinsic interest of this type of crime, enabled one to discern the overlap between such crimes and ordinary murders. The intimate connection between self-destructive and aggressive tendencies emerged clearly from the many incidents in which the offenders' intentions wavered uncertainly between murder and suicide. The same depressive and self-destructive factors were evident in many of the murderers who came to trial, especially those convicted for killing members of their family. But no simple descriptive formulation does justice to the variation and complexity of the human reactions involved in all these murders followed by suicide which, in particular instances, varied from coldly calculated murder for gain to impulsive destruction during the frantic agitation of a psychosis.

Tables

TABLE I

Annual number per 100,000 of population of:	Homicide offenders[1]	Homicide offenders who kill themselves	Suicides[2]	Suicide-[3] Murder Ratio
England and Wales	0·27	33% = 0·09	8·5	0·97
Denmark	0·53	42% = 0·22	21·0	0·98
U.S.A.	4·5 approx.	4% = 0·18	10·0	0·69
Australia	1·7	22% = 0·36	11·0	0·87

[1] Figures taken from Interpol: *International Crime Statistics* for years 1959–60.
[2] Figures for year 1959 taken from World Health Organization *Epidemiological and Vital Statistics*, 1961.
[3] This ratio represents the number of suicides divided by the total of suicides plus murders.

TABLE 2

SEX DISTRIBUTION OF OFFENDERS AND VICTIMS

Total Murder-Suicide Sample

	Offenders		Victims under 16 years		Victims 16 years or over		Total Victims	
	No.	%	No.	%	No.	%	No.	%
Male	88	59·5	42	46·2	14	14·6	56	29·9
Female	60	40·5	49	53·8	82	85·4	131	70·1
TOTAL	148	100	91	100	96	100	187	100
			Matched Murder Sample					
Male	138	88·5	13	46·4	43	33·6	56	35·9
Female	18	11·5	15	53·6	85	66·4	100	64·1
TOTAL	156	100	28	100	128	100	156	100

TABLE 3

AGE AND SEX OF OFFENDERS

Age of Offenders	Total Sample of 148 Murder-Suicide Offenders						Matching Sample of 156 murderers						National Sample of all murderers committed for trial 21 March 1957 to 31 December 1960[1]					
	Male		Female		Total		Male		Female		Total		Male		Female		Total	
	No.	%	No.	%	No.	%	No.	%	No.	%	No.	%	No.	%	No.	%	No.	%
Under 20 years	2	2·3	0	0	2	1·4	18	13·0	0	0	18	11·5	42	14·8	3	8·3	45	14·0
21 to 29	14	15·9	13	21·7	27	18·2	49	35·5	8	44·4	57	36·5	90	31·7	12	33·3	102	31·9
30 to 39	16	18·2	26	43·3	42	28·4	38	27·5	5	27·8	43	27·6	74	26·1	5	14·0	79	24·7
40 and over	56	63·6	21	35·0	77	52·0	33	24·0	5	27·8	38	24·4	78	27·4	16	44·4	94	29·4
TOTAL Offenders of known age	88	100	60	100	148	100	138	100	18	100	156	100	284	100	36	100	320	100

[1] See Gibson and Klein.

TABLE 4

AGE AND SEX OF VICTIMS

Age of Victims	Of 148 murderers who committed suicide						Of 156 surviving London murderers						Of Gibson and Klein's[1] national sample of all murderers, 21 March 1957 to 31 December 1960					
	Male		Female		Total		Male		Female		Total		Male		Female		Total	
	No.	%	No.	%	No.	%	No.	%	No.	%	No.	%	No.	%	No.	%	No.	%
Under 1 year	4	7·1	7	5·3	11	5·9	2	3·6	0	0	2	1·3	21	8·7	22	5·7	43	6·9
1 and under 5	16	28·6	18	13·7	34	18·2	7	12·5	9	9	16	10·3	35	14·4	37	9·7	72	11·5
5 and under 16	22	39·3	24	18·4	46	24·6	4	7·1	6	6	10	6·4	38	15·7	56	14·7	94	15·1
16 and under 30	3	5·4	28	21·4	31	16·6	8	14·3	23	23	31	19·8	41	17·0	64	16·7	105	16·8
30 and under 50	5	8·9	33	25·2	38	20·3	19	33·9	32	32	51	32·7	48	19·8	103	27·0	151	24·2
50 and over	6	10·7	21	16·0	27	14·4	16	28·6	30	30	46	29·5	59	24·4	100	26·2	159	25·5
TOTAL	56	100	131	100	187	100	56	100	100	100	156	100	242	100	382	100	624	100

[1] op. cit.

TABLE 5

AGE RANGES OF MURDER-SUICIDE OFFENDERS
AND OF SUICIDES

Percentage in age range:	Under 35 years	35 to 54 years	55 years and over
Male murder-suicide offenders	30	47	23
Male suicides in England and Wales[1]	14	37	49
Female murder-suicide offenders	56	29	15
Female suicides in England and Wales[1]	10	37	53

[1] *W.H.O. Epidemiological and Vital Statistics Report*, 1961, No. 14, p. 64

TABLE 6

RELATIONSHIP OF MURDERERS TO THEIR VICTIMS

| | 148 Murderers who committed suicide | | | | 156 Murderers brought to trial | | | | National Sample (Gibson and Klein) 320 Murderers in 1959 and 1960, convicted, insane or 'diminished responsibility' | | | |
| | Male | | Female | | Male | | Female | | Male | | Female | |
	No.	%	No.	%	No.	%	No.	%	No.	%	No.	%
Own children or spouse and children	15[1]	17·1	55[2]	91·7	11[7]	8·0	13	72·2	25	8·8	23	63·9
Spouse only	40[3]	45·5	3	5·0	26	18·9	1	5·6	52	18·3	5	13·9
Girl-friend/lover	21[4]	23·8	0	0	21	15·2	0	0	27	9·5	2	5·6
Other relative	6[5]	6·8	2	3·3	14	10·1	2	11·0	27	9·5	1	2·8
Acquaintances, etc.	2[6]	2·3	0	0	27[8]	19·6	1	5·6	38	13·4	3	8·3
Other	4	4·5	0	0	39	28·2	1	5·6	115	40·5	2	5·6
TOTAL	88	100	60	100	138	100	18	100	284	100	36	100

[1] One man in this category killed an adopted child.
[2] All of these killed only their children, 53 killed their children under 16 years.
[3] One killed a divorced wife.
[4] One also killed the girl-friend's father.
[5] One also killed his wife.
[6] One also killed a stranger.
[7] One killed both son and mother-in-law.
[8] Includes two who killed fellow mental patients in hospital and one who killed a homosexual associate.

TABLE 7

METHODS BY WHICH VICTIMS WERE KILLED[1]

	148 murder-suicide incidents								148 murder incidents brought to trial							
	Victims under 16 years		*Victims male, 16 or over*		*Victims female, 16 or over*		TOTAL *Victims*		*Victims under 16 years*		*Victims male, 16 or over*		*Victims female, 16 or over*		TOTAL *Victims*	
	No.	%	No.	%	No.	%	No.	%	No.	%	No.	%	No.	%	No.	%
Stabbing, use of sharp instrument	3	3	1	7	18	22	22	11·7	2	7	14	33	27	32	43	27·6
Blows, kicks, use of blunt instruments	0	0	1	7	8	9	9	4·8	3	11	14	33	17	20	34	21·8
Strangulation, asphyxiation	2	2	0	0	18	22	20	10·7	14	50	4	9	40	47	58	37·2
Gas poisoning	80	87	2	14	10	12	92	49·2	6	21	1	2	0	0	7	4·5
Shooting	3	3	10	71	24	31	37	19·8	0	0	7	16	1	1	8	5·1
Other methods, e.g. drugs	4	4	0	0	3	4	7	3·7	3	11	3	7	0	0	6	3·8
TOTAL	92	100	14	100	81	100	187	100	28	100	43	100	85	100	156	100

[1] Counting only the chief cause of death in each victim.

DISTRIBUTION OF OFFENDERS BY MARITAL STATUS, COMPARED WITH
GENERAL POPULATION AND SAINSBURY'S SAMPLE OF LONDON SUICIDES

	Married		Single		Separated or Divorced		Widowed		Not Known		TOTAL	
	No.	%	No.	%	No.	%	No.	%	No.	%	No.	%
FEMALES												
Total Murder-Suicide Sample	46	76·6	4	6·7	3	5·0	7	11·7	0	0	60	100
Murder Sample	15	83·3	1	5·6	1	5·6	1	5·6	0	0	18	100
1951 Census. Greater London, Females aged 20 or over		64·0		21·0		1·1		13·9				100
Sainsbury's sample of London Suicides[1]		45·4		34·8		5·3		14·4				100
MALES												
Total Murder-Suicide Sample	47	53·4	20	22·7	19	21·6	2	2·3	0	0	88	100
Murder Sample	39	28·2	71	51·5	24	17·5	2	1·4	2	1·4	138	100
1951 Census. Greater London, Males aged 15 or over		70·0		24·6		0·7		4·6		0		100
Sainsbury's sample of London Suicides[1]		43·7		24·9		5·4		13·3		12·6		100

[1] These percentages, given separately for males and females, are approximations derived from Table C, p. 66, using the ratios of male to female suicide rates quoted by Sainsbury to estimate the numbers of males and females. Those 'not known' were mostly living alone and presumably not married.

159

TABLE 9

MALE OFFENDERS BY SOCIO-ECONOMIC STATUS ON THE REGISTRAR-GENERAL'S CLASSIFICATION OF OCCUPATIONS, COMPARED WITH MALE SUICIDES AND MALE POPULATION

Social Class	Murder-Suicide Offenders		Murderers Tried		Suicides by Males aged 20–64 (Registrar-General)	1951 Census Occupied and retired males
	No.	%	No.	%	%	%
I	6	6·8	2	1·4	4·8	4·7
II	8	9·1	11	8·0	18·5	16·2
III	44	50·0	52	37·7	44·1	55·1
IV	12	13·6	28	20·3	14·1	10·7
V	7	8·0	35	25·4	16·2	13·3
Unclassified	11	12·5	10	7·2	2·2	—
TOTAL	88	100	138	100	100	100

TABLE 10

APPROXIMATE TIMES OF DAY OF MURDERS

Time of Day	Murder-Suicide Incidents			Murder Incidents		
	Male Offenders	*Female Offenders*	*All Offenders*	*Male Offenders*	*Female Offenders*	*All Offenders*
4.0 a.m. up to 10 a.m.	15	10	25	17	1	18
10 a.m. up to 4.0 p.m.	18	29	47	28	6	34
4.0 p.m. up to 10.0 p.m.	14	9	23	25	3	28
10.0 p.m. up to 4.0 a.m.	38	10	48	59	6	65
Not known	3	2	5	1	2	3
TOTAL	88	60	148	130	18	148

TABLE 11

DAYS OF THE WEEK ON WHICH INCIDENTS TOOK PLACE

	Mon.	*Tues.*	*Wed.*	*Thurs.*	*Fri.*	*Sat.*	*Sun.*	*Not known*
148 murders followed by suicide	37	26	14	18	26	19	6	2
148 murder incidents	22	18	20	17	24	22	25	0

TABLE 12

PERCENTAGES OF MURDERS, MURDER-SUICIDES AND SUICIDES FALLING INTO EACH OF FOUR SEASONAL QUARTERS

	Mar.Apr.May	Jun.Jul.Aug.	Sept.Oct.Nov.	Dec.Jan.Feb.
National sample of murders (N=1314)	29·6	23·9	23·8	22·6
Murders followed by suicide (N=148)	27·0	35·1	15·6	22·3
Suicides in the United Kingdom (W.H.O.)	27·6	24·7	23·6	24·0

TABLE 13

PREVIOUS CONVICTIONS

	148 Murderers who killed themselves				156 Murderers brought to trial and not acquitted			
	Male		Female		Male		Female	
	No.	%	No.	%	No.	%	No.	%
No previous conviction	71	80·7	58	96·7	66	47·8	16	88·9
One or more previous convictions known to be for violence against persons	7	8·0	1	1·7	21	15·2	0	0
Previously convicted but not for violence	10	11·3	1	1·7	51	37·0	2	11·1
TOTAL	88	100	60	100	138	100	18	100

TABLE 14

MENTAL STATE OF 78 MURDER-SUICIDE OFFENDERS[1]

Relatively 'Normal' Offenders		Depressives (psychotic or severe reactive)		Schizophrenics		Morbid Jealousy		Psychopaths		Markedly Neurotic or Unstable	
Male	Female	Male	Female	Male	Female	Male	Female	Male	Female	Male	Female
(1) (2) (4) (5) (8) (12) (15) (18) (24) (29) (30) (32) (41) (43) (46) (51) (54) (59) (64) (65) (67) (72) (73) (78)	(13) (19) (21) (28) (39) (49) (55) (74) (75)	(3) (9) (27) (33) (45) (63) (68)	(6) (7) (11) (16) (17) (23) (26) (31) (34) (35) (37) (42) (44) (47) (50) (52) (53) (56) (62) (71) (77)	(48) (66)	(25) (69)	(10) (61)		(17) (22)[2] (40)[2] (57)		(14)[2] (36) (58)[2] (60) (76)[2]	(38)[2] (70)
TOTAL Offenders = 24	9	7	21	2	2	2	0	4	0	5	2

Total abnormal offenders: 20 males and 25 females.

[1] The numbers in brackets refer to individual case numbers.

[2] The 6 offenders thus marked were considered to be insufficiently disturbed to be found 'insane' or of 'diminished responsibility' had they come before a jury.

TABLE 15

METHODS OF KILLING USED BY 78 MURDER-SUICIDE OFFENDERS

	Methods used by 39 'insane' offenders		Methods used by 39 'sane' offenders	
	Males	*Females*	*Males*	*Females*
Stabbing. Sharp instruments	4	2	6	0
Blows, kicks, blunt instrument, etc.	3	0	3	0
Strangling. Asphyxiation	3	0	6	0
Coal gas poisoning	4	21	6	9
Shooting	3	0	11	1
Other methods (including drugs)	1	2	2	1
TOTAL	18	25	34	11
Number of offenders who used two methods	3	1	5	1

TABLE 16

AGE DISTRIBUTION OF DEPRESSIVE OFFENDERS
IN THE MAIN MURDER-SUICIDE SAMPLE

Percentage in Age ranges:	Under 40 years	40 to 49 years	50 and over
All admissions for manic-depressive psychosis in 1959	24	20	56
First admissions for manic-depressive psychosis in 1959	31	20	49
21 depressive female offenders[1]	71 (N=15)	25 (N=5)	5 (N=1)
7 depressive male offenders[1]	29 (N=2)	15 (N=1)	57 (N=4)

[1] The percentages in the last two rows, being based on very small numbers, are unreliable, but they show the direction of the trend.

TABLE 17

KILLINGS IN THE EARLY MORNING BY 78
MURDER-SUICIDE OFFENDERS

	No. of murders by depressive offenders	No. of murders by other offenders	TOTAL
Murder between 4.0 a.m. and 10.0 a.m.	7	6	13
Murder at other times, or times unknown	21	44	65
TOTAL	28	50	78

TABLE 18

METHODS OF SUICIDE

	Percentage using Active Methods		Percentage using Passive Methods	
	Males	*Females*	*Males*	*Females*
Murder-Suicide Cases (N = 148)	65	10	35	90
Capstick's[1] Sample of Suicides (N = 881)	70	38	30	62

[1] op. cit.

TABLE 19

SANE AND INSANE OFFENDERS CONTRASTED

No. of offenders with:	39 'Sane' Offenders	39 'Insane' Offenders
Previous suicidal attempts	9	4
Time lapse before suicide more than one day	2	0
Manifest hostility to victim the prime motive	10	3
Extended suicide the prime motive	19	25

TABLE 20

DEATH RATES PER 100,000 POPULATION
FOR YEAR 1960[1]

Country	Suicide and Self-Inflicted Injury	Homicide and Operations of War
Eire	3·0	0·2
Denmark	20·3	0·5
England and Wales	11·2	0·6
Switzerland	19·0	0·6
Belgium	14·6	0·7
West Germany	18·8	1·0
Canada	7·6	1·4
Australia	10·6	1·5
Italy	6·3	1·5
France	15·9	1·7
Japan	21·2	1·9
Finland	20·4	2·9
Ceylon	9·9	3·3
U.S.A.	10·8	4·5
Venezuela	6·6	8·7

[1] Data taken from World Health Organization *Epidemiological and Vital Statistics*, 1962, No. 15, p. 519.

TABLE 21[1]

Number of countries with:	Low suicide rate, *i.e.* 5·0 or less	High suicide rate, *i.e.* 12·0 or more	Totals of 36 Countries
High homicide rate, i.e. 3·5 or more	8	1	13
Low homicide rate, i.e. 1·0 or less	2	5	13
Totals of 36 countries	10	11	

[1] Adapted from A. L. Wood, op. cit.

References

References

Alexander, F. and Staub, H., *The Criminal, the Judge, and the Public*, Revised Ed., Glencoe, Ill., 1956

Baker, J., 'Female Criminal Lunatics', *Journ. Mental Science*, 1902, 48, 13–28

Banay, R. S., 'Study in Murder', *Annals Amer. Ac. Polit. Soc. Sc.*, 1952, 284, 26–34

Bandura, A. and Walters, R. H., *Adolescent Aggression*, New York, 1959, p. 121

Banen, D. M., 'Suicide by Psychotics', *Journ. Nerv. and Mental Disease*, 1954, 120, 349–57

Batchelor, I. R. C., 'Psychopathic states and attempted suicide', *Brit. Medical Journ.*, 1954, 1, 1342–7

Batchelor, I. R. C., 'Alcohol and attempted suicide', *Journ. Mental Science*, 1954, 100, 451–61

Batt, J. C., 'Homicidal Incidence in the Depressive Psychoses', *Journ. Mental Science*, 1948, 94, 782–92

Bender, L., 'Psychiatric Mechanisms in Child Murderers', *Journ. Nervous and Mental Dis.*, 1934, 80, 32–47

Berkowitz, L., (Ed.), *Aggression*, New York, 1962

Brearley, H. C., *Homicide in the U.S.A.*, Chapel Hill, N.C., 1932

Bruhn, J. G., 'A comparative study of attempted suicides and psychiatric out-patients', *Brit. Journ. Preventive Soc. Medicine*, 1963, 17, 197–201

Campbell, J. D., *Manic-Depressive Disease*, Philadelphia and London, 1953

Capstick, A., 'Urban and rural suicide', *Journ. Mental Science*, 1960, 106, 1327–36

Capstick, A., 'Recognition of emotional disturbance and the prevention of suicide', *Brit. Medical Journ.*, 1960, i, 1179–82

Cavan, R., *Suicide*, Chicago, 1928

Christie, T., 'The Manic-Depressive Psychoses in relation to Crime', *Medico-Legal Journ.*, 1942, 10, 10–21

Citterio, C., *et al.*, 'Psicosi depressive e criminalità', *Il Lavoro Neuropsichiatrico*, 1962, 31, 1–15

Cohen, J., 'A study of suicide pacts', *Medico-Legal Journ.*, 1961, 29, 144–51

Dollard, J., *et al.*, *Frustration and Aggression*, London, 1944

Durkheim, E., *Suicide* (transl.), London, 1952

East, W. Norwood, 'On attempted suicide', *Journ. Mental Science*, 1913, 59, 428

East, W. Norwood, *Introduction to Forensic Psychiatry*, London, 1927

East, W. Norwood, *Medical Aspects of Crime*, London, 1936

East, W. Norwood, *Society and the Criminal*, London, 1949

Fantl, B. and Schiro, J., 'Cultural variables in the behaviour of . . . Schizophrenics', *Internat. J. Soc. Psychiatry*, 1959, 4, 245–53

Fenichel, O., *The Psycho-analytic Theory of Neurosis*, London, 1945

Ferri, E., *L'Omicida—L'Omicidio Suicidio*, Turin, 1925

Fuentes, C. R., 'Statistical information', *Internat. Criminal Police Rev.*, 1961, No. 148, 145–9

Gibbens, T. C. N., 'Sane and Insane Homicide', *Journ. Criminal Law, Criminol. and Police Science*, 1958, 49, 110–15

Gibbs, J. P. 'Suicide' in R. K. Merton and R. A. Nisbet *Contemporary Social Problems*, New York, 1961

Gibson, E. and Klein, S., *Murder*, London, H.M.S.O., 1961

Gold, M., 'Suicide, homicide and aggression', *Amer. Journ. Sociol.*, 1958, 63, 651–61

Gould, J., 'The Psychiatry of Major Crime', *Recent Progress in Psychiatry* (Ed. G. W. T. H. Fleming), 1959, 3, 303–51

Grunhut, M., 'Murder and the death penalty in England', *Annals Amer. Acad. Polit. and Soc. Sc.*, 1952, 284, 158–66

Halbwachs, M., *Les causes du Suicide*, Paris, 1930

Harlan, H., 'Five hundred homicides', *Journ. Crim. Law, Criminol. and Police Sc.*, 1950, 40, 736–52

Havard, J. D. J., *The Detection of Secret Homicide*, London, 1960

Henderson, D. K. and Gillespie, R. D., *Textbook of Psychiatry*, Oxford, 1947

Hendin, H., 'Suicide in Sweden', *Psychiatric Quarterly*, 1962, 36, 1–28

Hendin, H., 'Suicide in Denmark', *Psychiatric Quarterly*, 1960, 34, 443–60

Henry, A. F. and Short, J., *Suicide and Homicide*, Glencoe, Ill., 1954

Hoffman, F. L., *The Homicide Problem*, Newark, 1925

Hopwood, J. S., 'Child murder and insanity', *Journ. Mental Science*, 1927, 73, 95–108

Hurwitz, S., *Criminology* (2nd Ed. Transl. Giersing), London, 1952

Illinois Crime Survey, Chicago Crime Commission, 1929, p. 612

Jervis, J., *The Office and Duties of Coroners* (9th Ed.), London, 1957

Kessel, N., et al., 'Attempted suicide in Edinburgh', *Scot. Medical Journ.*, 1962, 7, 130–5

Kiloh, L. G. and Garside, R. F., 'The independence of neurotic depression and endogenous depression', *Brit. Journ. Psychiatry*, 1963, 109, 451–63

Kraepelin, E., *Manic-Depressive Insanity and Paranoia* (transl. R. M. Barclay), Edinburgh, 1921

Kraines, S. H., *Mental Depressions and their Treatment*, New York, 1957

Lanzkron, J., 'Murder and Insanity', *Amer. Journ. Psychiatry*, 1963, 119, 754–8

Lithner, F., 'Mord och ajalvmord', *Nord T. Kriminalvidensk*, 1962, 50, 280–95

McDermaid, G. and Winkler, E. G., 'Psychiatric study of homicide cases' *Journ. Clinical Psycho-pathology*, 1950, 11, 93–146

McGrath, P. G., Personal Communication (Based on a talk at the Quarterly Meeting of the Royal Medico-Psychological Assn., May 1963)

McKenzie, R. W., Personal communication (thesis), 1961

Menninger, F., *Man Against Himself*, New York, 1938

Mohr, J. W., 'Prison or Hospital', *Canadian Psychiatric Assn. Journ.*, 1964, 9, 101–10

Morris, T. and Blom-Cooper, L., *A Calendar of Murder*, London, 1964

Morselli, H., *Suicide* (transl.), New York, 1882

Morton, J. H., 'Female Homicides', *Journ. Mental Science*, 1934, 80, 64–74

Neiberg, N. A., 'Murder and Suicide', *Archiv. Criminal Psychodynamics*, 1961, 4, 253–68

Neustatter, W. L., 'Psychiatric Aspects of Diminished Responsibility in Murder', *Medico-Legal Journ.*, 1960, 28, 92–101

Opler, M., *et al.*, 'Ethnic differences in behaviour and psychopathology', *Internat. J. Soc. Psychiatry*, 1956, 2, 11–22

Parnell, R. W. and Skottowe, I., 'Towards preventing suicide', *Lancet*, 1957, i, 206–8

Porterfield, A. L., 'Indices of homicide and suicide by states and cities', *Amer. Sociol. Rev.*, 1949, 14, 481–90

Porterfield, A. L., 'Traffic fatalities, suicide and homicide' *Amer. Sociol. Rev.*, 1960, 25, 897–901

Rabin, A. I., 'Homicide and attempted suicide', *Amer. Journ. Orthopsychiatry*, 1946, 16, 516–24

Sainsbury, P., *Suicide in London*, London, 1955

Sears, R. R., 'Relation of early socialisation experiences to aggression', *Journ. Abnormal and Social Psychol.*, 1961, 63, 461–5

Sellin, Thorsten, *The Death Penalty*, Philadelphia, 1959

Selzer, M. L. and Payne, C. E., 'Automobile Accidents, Suicide and Alcoholism', *Proc. 3rd Internat. Conf. on Alcohol and Road Traffic*, London, 1962, 104–7

Siciliano, S., 'Resultati preliminari di un 'indagine sull 'omicido in Danimarca', *Scuola Positiva*, 1961, 718–29

Sparks, R. F., 'Diminished Responsibility in Theory and Practice', *Modern Law Review*, 1964, 27, 9–34

Stengel, E. and Cook, N. G., *Attempted Suicide*, London, 1958

Sullivan, W. C., *Crime and Insanity*, London, 1924

Tarde, G., *Penal Philosophy* (transl.), Boston, 1912

Thurston, G., *Coroner's Practice*, London, 1958

Tillman, W. A. and Hobbs, G. E., 'The accident-prone and automobile driver', *Amer. Journ. Psychiatry*, 1949, 106, 321–31

Walton, H. J., 'Suicidal behaviour in Depressive Illness', *Journ. Mental Science*, 1958, 104, 884–91

Wertham, F., *The Show of Violence*, New York and London, 1949

Whitlock, F. A., *Criminal Responsibility and Mental Illness*, London, 1963

Willett, T. C., *Criminal on the Road*, London, 1964

Williams, A. Hyatt, 'The psychopathology of sexual murderers',
I. Rosen (Ed.), *The Pathology and Treatment of Sexual Deviation*, London, 1964

Wily, H. J. and Stallworthy, K. R., *Mental Abnormality and the Law*, Christchurch, N.Z., 1962

Woddis, G. M., 'Depression and Crime', *Brit. Journ. Delinquency*, 1957, 8, 85–94

Wolfgang, M. E., 'An Analysis of Homicide-Suicide', *Journ. Clinical and Exptl. Psychopathology*, 1958, 19, 208–18

Wood, A. L., 'Crime and Aggression in Ceylon', *Trans. Am. Phil. Soc.*, 1961, 51, pt. 8

World Health Organization, *Epidemiological and Vital Statistics Report*, 1961, 24, Nos. 5, 12

Zilborg, G., 'Differential diagnosis of types of suicides', *Archiv. Neurol. and Psychiat.*, 1936, 35, 270–91

Appendix

LIST OF CASES CITED IN THE TEXT

Case Numbers   **Page Numbers**

Case Numbers	Page Numbers
2	23, 58, 61, 127
3	116
4	49, 60
5	49, 73, 128
6	72
7	70, 148
8	58
9	49, 107, 108
10	64, 81
12	59, 127
13	50, 84
14	85, 128, 146
15	48, 49, 73
16	69, 148
18	58
20	83, 146
22	59, 65, 82
23	75
24	60
25	80
27	71, 108
28	49, 74, 84
29	49
31	49, 74
32	49
33	71, 108, 112, 128
34	108
35	20, 105, 108
36	86

* These cases are not included in the samples, nor in the tabulations.

Index

accidental death, 18–19
age distribution and range of
offenders and victims, 29–
30, 43; tables 2, 3, 4, 5,
16; of depressive offenders,
102–3
aged persons as offenders, 4,
55
aggression, 5; murder and suicide as alternative forms of,
4–6, 23, 113–26; in neurotic
and psychopathic offenders,
85–6; theories of, 94–8;
and melancholia, 102–8
passim; social status as important factor in degrees of,
131–42 passim; in killings
by the insane, 149; con-
nection with self-destructive motives, 150
agitated depression as prelude
to suicide, 107–9
alcoholism and drug-taking as
factors in homicide inci-
dents, 34, 41, 43, 49, 60,
86, 90, 117, 121, 124–5
altruistic killings, 6–7, 10, 48,
92–4, 97, 98, 133–4, 149:
see also 'mercy killings'
anxiety-neurosis, theory of, 5
Australia
homicide statistics and records,
7, 8, table 1; death rates
(from violence), table 20

Belgium, death rates (from
violence) in, table 20
Broadmoor Hospital
murder followed by attempted
suicide among inmates of,
2–3; diagnosis of mental
illness in, 88

Canada, death rates (from
violence) in, table 20
Capital Murder, definition, 37
'catathymic crisis' in psychotic
outbursts, 101
Ceylon
death rates (from violence) in,
table 20; effects of varying
economic and social status
in killings in, 137
child-rearing practices
as factor leading to suicide,
120–1; effects of varying
customs in, 139–40
child victims, 27–9 passim, 38,
42, 44, 45, 50–1, 53, 62, 65,
85, 98, 101, 102, 109, 141,
145, 147, 148–9
criminal types and offenders
with previous convictions,
36–9, 42, 44, 57, 62, table
13; among murder-suicides,
56–62, 145; as risk-takers
in road-accident incidents,
125–6

177